C0-CZY-052

The Bride's Book Of Showers

The Bride's Book Of Showers

By Ginny Hopkins

GROSSET & DUNLAP

A NATIONAL GENERAL COMPANY

Publishers • New York

FOR JACK AND LISA

Portions of this book appeared in
Modern Bride © 1967 by Ziff-Davis
Publishing Company, and *Lady's Circle*
© 1968 by Lady's Circle Incorporated

Copyright © 1971 by Ginny Hopkins

All Rights Reserved

Published Simultaneously in Canada
Library of Congress Catalog Card Number: 75–144070
SBN: 448–02224–9
PRINTED IN THE UNITED STATES OF AMERICA

FOREWORD

Why do we love this book of showers? Because whether you and your friends are about to be married and start a new life, or whether you are beginning a family of your own, you'll be celebrating the happy occasion with relatives and friends. And since their good wishes are so often expressed in the thoughtful giving of some small necessity, a gala atmosphere should surround the receiving of them. Gifts may be given with grace in any setting—from the pink tablecloths and pink plastic rain that once were traditional shower decor to the contemporary excitement of psychedelic colors. Ginny Hopkins' book is full of ideas for these as well as a thousand surprises to shower on a bride, prospective mother, or other recipient. The unexpected is everywhere: in the completeness of the shopping lists, in the wide range of party themes and correspondingly imaginative decor, in the thoroughgoing gift suggestions, in the careful attention to the one detail—budget—so often overlooked in books dedicated to lavish entertaining.

It is with great pleasure then that we associate ourselves with what must surely become the definitive work on showers. We wish you many happy hours reading its pages and enjoying the parties that follow. May its ideas color your entertaining style, happily ever after.

Barbara Donovan
Editor-in-Chief
THE BRIDE'S MAGAZINE

PREFACE

There's no better reason for giving a party than to have a shower. Elegant or casual, large or small, for distaffers or including the men, showers are fun.

Showers are not new on the entertainment scene, but that doesn't mean they have to be formalized repetitions of the gift-game-refreshments syndrome that's been traditional for far too long. These days showers are limited only by the hostess' imagination and inventiveness, and just about anything in good taste goes.

The purpose of this book is to provide ideas on types of showers, suggest gifts, themes, plans and menus. They are adaptable, so add or subtract, revise and delete to suit yourself. These parties do not need cutesy invitations or party games. They do depend upon congenial friends, good food and drinks, carefully chosen gifts.

There is one thing missing—the particular plus of your own personality, the stamp of individuality that only you can provide. So use your imagination to build your own brand of parties on the superstructures you'll find here.

Happy entertaining!

Contents

Contents

Parties . . . Cocktail Party . . . Eggnog . . . Sherry . . . Apéritif . . . Liqueur . . . Italian Dinner . . . Scandinavian Buffet . . . Oriental Buffet Dinner . . . Hawaiian Luau . . . Progressive Dinner . . . Cookout . . . Picnics . . . Swim Party . . . Box Supper . . . Restaurant Party . . . Dessert Only . . . Cheese and Wine Tasting . . . Evening Punch . . . Late Night Supper

Contents

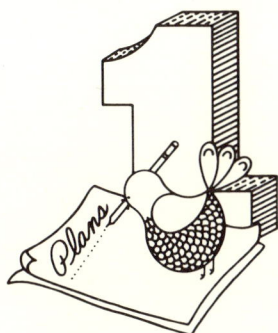

Planning Your Party

Good parties don't just happen. They're the result of careful attention to detail. So when you decide to give a shower, the first thing to do is get out a pad and pencil and plan, plan, plan.

Who gives a shower? Just about any interested hostess except a member of the honorée's family. If an aunt, grandmother or other close relative wants to give a shower, however, she may do so if she limits the guests to family members only. Aside from this one limitation, intimate friends, sorority sisters, business associates, fellow club members, office co-workers, any or all may want to celebrate a momentous occasion by giving a shower.

To limit the number of showers and, coincidentally, the financial burden on the guests, several hostesses can go together for one smashing party, dividing the work and the expense. Give it in the largest house and make different gals responsible for food, invitations and gifts, table settings, decorations, entertainment and cleaning up.

Always keep in mind the taste, interests and needs of the honor guest and be sure the theme calls for gifts that are useful yet relatively inexpensive. This is especially important if some of the same people are being invited to more than one party for the same gal. Your own gift is usually the container in which the packages are presented, so be sure it matches the shower theme.

Be wary of traditional shower games and don't plan any unless you're sure your guests really enjoy them. The parties outlined here are strong enough to stand on their own.

If it's an all girl party, just conversation which gives the guests a chance to catch up on everyone's comings and goings is entertainment enough. If you've invited the men, plan the same sort of evening you usually enjoy when the gang gets together. If the shower is of a type men don't enjoy, consider asking them to come in later, after the gift opening but before the food.

Delegate one person to record the gifts and keep the cards with them. If you can, have the gifts delivered before party time so they can be arranged attractively in advance. Otherwise, have the guests arrive about half an hour before the guest of honor so you can attend to the packages then.

If the shower is a secret, say so on the invitation. You've probably already discovered that surprises of this sort rarely come off, and many people go as far as to consider them positively horrendous.

"Surprise" showers rarely catch the honor guest completely unaware, but she still feels she should simper foolishly, "Why, is this really a party for little ole me?" Spare everyone by telling her in advance. This way, too, you can find out exactly what she wants and needs without subterfuge, trickery or, worse yet, exposing the secret prematurely.

Be sure invitations go only to really good friends. It's embarrassing for a casual acquaintance to feel put on the spot and equally awkward for the guest of honor to accept a gift from her. Scrutinize the guest list carefully to be sure no one is overlooked and to avoid uncongenial people. If a lot of parties are being given, limit the guests to those who haven't been asked several times before or choose an inexpensive theme. Remember, the purpose of the shower is to fete your friend, not bankrupt your guests.

One other warning: the shower is to enable friends to share a particularly significant event. Don't use a shower to repay your own party obligations or to introduce a new friend to your group.

The kind of party you plan depends upon the kind you like to give and do best. Accept your limitations and consider your budget, the capacity of your home and its facilities.

Being sensible doesn't mean you can't be creative. It does mean you should keep the party in line with the way you live, your own style and your entertaining experience.

Once you've decided on the time and kind of party, don't trust instinct or memory. Write everything down. Make lists of guests, gifts, food, beverages, decorations and equipment. Let even your lists have lists!

Try not to borrow anything. If a borrowed item is lost or damaged, you'll have to replace it. So it's smarter to buy your own things if you can. Otherwise, consider renting. Almost everything from coffee urns to table napkins can be rented for modest fees these days.

Make a detailed master plan and timetable for finishing each job. Work ahead as much as you can. Check your linens, silver and other equipment to be sure it's immaculate. And if you're getting out seldom used china or crystal wash it a couple of days before the party so it will be sparkling. Decide what you'll wear and be sure your clothes are ready early. Do staple food shopping a week in advance, then pick up perishable items the day before the party.

Be sure to have an outside light to welcome guests to after-dark parties, adequate space for wraps, enough chairs, lots of large ashtrays in convenient places, several brands of cigarettes in containers, plenty of matches or lighters, and soft lighting. If you plan to play cards have auxiliary lamps standing by. Stock a guest spot in the bathroom with facial tissues, hand towels, powder puffs, hand lotion, an extra comb, individual guest soaps and a spare roll of bathroom tissue.

A successful party giver heeds certain *don'ts* as well as the more obvious *do's*. Don't spend the day of the party cooking and cleaning and don't choose menus that call for more than one or two complicated jobs to be done at the last minute. Don't leave advance jobs until the last minute—clean fruits and vegetables and do cutting, stewing, marinating, whatever, ahead so the kitchen will be cleared

5

for action early party morning. Clean the house thoroughly a day or two before. Then a light dusting, once over the bathroom and setting the rooms in order is all you'll need to do.

During the party don't rush around too much with ashtrays, matches, drinks or food. Don't insist people drink alcoholic beverages or eat more than they want to. And don't coax guests to stay longer or hold them up at the door with lengthy good-byes.

Above all, don't let an emergency throw you. Ignore it if you can. If you can't, deal with it as unobtrusively as possible. Treat it casually and so will your guests. Overreact and so will they.

The guest also has a part in making a party successful. Not all the people at a shower may know each other, so don't huddle with your own clique and turn the others off. Circulate and, if necessary, give the hostess a hand by introducing yourself and mixing with those who may otherwise feel like outsiders.

It is not necessary to send a gift if you don't go to a shower. A polite refusal is enough. However, if you like, send your present to the hostess ahead of the party. Remember, too, that a shower gift does not take the place of a wedding gift. You can, however, make the shower gift modest, even a token, and still be in good taste.

It's nice but not absolutely necessary for guests to phone the hostess a day or so after the party to thank her. But the guest of honor should send thank you notes—to the hostess for the party and to the guests for the gifts. Busy though she may be, she won't want to neglect this detail which is, after all, another gracious gesture that comes from a friendly heart.

Wedding Showers– for Him and Her

Happy indeed is the bride who's caught in a shower. Dowries are pretty much a thing of the past, and the shower takes the place of a hope chest for most of today's brides. Which means things haven't changed as much as you might think, for it was just such a situation that inspired the first wedding shower.

Legend has it that years and years ago a young Dutch girl was in love with the proverbial poor young man. In fact, he was so generous to others that he couldn't seem to accumulate a fortune of his own. Because of this lack of wealth the girl's father considered her lover a poor marriage prospect and he refused to give them a dowry. Sympathetic villagers decided to help the young couple by making up the dowry themselves. Each person gave a treasured possession of his own until they had contributed all the household goods a bride was expected to bring to her new home.

Since today's bride is more likely to bring education and job skills to her new husband than a full complement of household and personal items, she may need a shower nearly as desperately as did that legendary Dutch bride. Regardless of her needs, she'll treasure the feeling behind a prenuptial shower.

In addition to close friends, it's customary to include members of the wedding party and the mothers of the bride and bridegroom, unless the party is given by an office staff, sorority or other special interest group. Be sure that no one receives a shower invitation if she has not been invited to the wedding. Unless, of course, the ceremony is limited to families only. A "family only" shower given by a relative of the bride is a marvelous chance for the women of both families to get to know each other socially.

While in the past showers were limited to the ladies, there's no reason today not to include the men. For if the gifts rain on the bridegroom too, you'd be surprised what a swinging affair it can become.

Be sure, though, that the party theme is appropriate for couples. This is no time for intimate gifts. Instead, consult the couple on what they really want, then choose a theme that fits their needs. Combine with good food, good drinks and fun for a party they'll all remember.

If you do plan to invite men as well as women to your wedding shower—and we hope you'll do more and more of this—be sure the party is one which will appeal to both.

The rule of thumb is whether or not the bridegroom will be able to use the gifts. If he can (and this includes pots and pans), then chances are the males will enjoy choosing gifts and congratulating the groom on the acquisitions to the new household.

A shower should be fun as a party, not just a way to give gifts. And it will be, if you set out to make it so.

All of the showers in this section are suited to mixed groups, though they can also be given for women only. So take the ideas, make them your own and gain a reputation for giving the best showers in town!

Entertainment Shower

Hospitality helpers loom large in the newly married picture, so give a shower of accessories that will provide entertaining equipment for years to come.

If the bride belongs to a club, if the bridegroom plays cards with a regular group, or the two play bridge or pinochle, their cohorts can give them a party with gifts geared to their mutual interest. Or this is a good chance for old friends to wish the couple happiness with special gifts they can share later.

If this party is given by a regular group, have the kind of party they always enjoy. If it's a gathering of old friends try something less familiar—a coffee-tasting evening or Sunday brunch.

Stretch a flower-twined table tennis net across the serving table and use the game theme whenever you can: throw dice to see who starts the line at the buffet table, cut sandwiches and cookies in heart, diamond, spade and club shapes, and use paper napkins and coasters with playing card symbols.

A card table and folding chairs or a chafing dish and tray could be a gift from the group. Or several guests can chip in to buy season tickets, museum memberships or an electric carving knife, while others choose their gifts from this list:

    quilted plastic card table covers
    decks of cards
    score pads and pencils
    card shuffler
    games for two (such as cribbage)
    games for a group (such as Monopoly)
    dice
    poker chips and holder
    roulette wheel
    badminton, croquet or table tennis equipment
    movie script books
    membership in a local museum
    tickets for plays, concerts or sports events
    personalized matches, napkins and coasters
    oversize salad serving bowl
    fondue pot
    nest of individual salad bowls
    cheese board and cutter
    guest towels
    guest soaps
    cocktail picks

swizzle sticks
pickle fork
mustard spoon
colored toothpicks
electric warming tray
popcorn popper

Pack the gifts in a cardboard storage chest, set them up on a card or game table or wheel them in on a mobile server.

China and Glass Shower

Since crystal and fine china are expensive shower gifts, it makes more financial sense to concentrate on the day-to-day aspects of married life with shower gifts of everyday china and glass.

Invite a crowd for a late afternoon cocktail party or for dessert and coffee. Use your own china and glass as much as possible: flowers in crystal vases, massed in glass pitchers or floated in shallow dessert bowls. Utilize glass or china servers for beverages, sugar and cream and fill pretty china bowls with nuts, chips and heaps of matches. Your table centerpiece can be built around small glass animals and china figurines or flowers in glass containers.

The group can go together to buy basic place settings of earthenware or pottery, some good-looking yet practical sets of glasses of various sizes and styles or special sets of salad or dessert plates.

Or ask your friends to bring individual gifts, such as:

decorative bottles—some of the best finds are in thrift shops
salt and pepper shakers
ashtrays
candle holders
tile trivet
decanter
candy dish
compote
pitcher
hourglass egg timer
decorative or serving bowls
one-of-a-kind liqueur glasses

cruets
sugar bowl
cream pitcher
vase
mustard jar
figurine
paperweight
breakfast plates
coffee mugs
demitasse cups and saucers
pair of ceramic napkin rings
oven-proof glass casseroles
glass or china flowers
ceramic light-switch plates
individual salt and pepper shakers

Create a glass and china "shop" for the gifts by arranging the packages in an empty bookcase or on small "display" tables, or erect temporary shelves by placing boards on stacks of books to the height you need.

Bar Shower

Definitely for couples, this party will set the newlyweds up with the bar basics they'll need, whether it's cocktails for two or drinks for a mob.

Plan a Sunday breakfast, a buffet dinner, a cheese-tasting party or an evening of cards or dancing. If the weather is right, consider a swim party or picnic. Serve drinks by all means, but observe one unbreakable rule: under no circumstances will the guests be allowed to drink *any* of the bride and groom's new booze.

Perhaps the fathers-in-law can be prevailed upon to donate an electric blender and an electric ice crusher. Several couples might want to pool their funds for these or other of the more expensive gifts, such as a punch bowl and ladle.

Any of the following will be equally welcome:

bottles of bourbon, Scotch, rye, gin, vodka or brandy
wine, liqueur

various mixes
decanter
cocktail shaker
Martini pitcher
serving trays
cocktail, highball, wine, liqueur, beer, or brandy glasses
punch cups
beer steins
ice bucket
ice tongs
aerosol "icer" for champagne and cocktail glasses
gadget that converts tap water into club soda
wine rack
wine basket
jigger measure
permanent bottle caps
bar strainer
corkscrew
bar knife
long-handled bar mixing spoon
lime or lemon squeezer
terrycloth bar towels
cocktail picks
coasters
cocktail napkins—paper or linen
huge ashtrays
matches
bottles of cocktail olives, pearl onions and maraschino cherries
divided snack dishes
cans of peanuts and mixed nuts
bowls for dips and snacks
bartender's apron
book of drink recipes

Set the wrapped gift packages on an improvised bar fashioned from an emptied bookcase or a sheet-draped ironing board.

Candle Shower

While the romantic aspects of dining by candlelight have been well documented, there are many other kinds and types of candles that will help the couple live in style.

Give an evening party and use candles for all the lighting, not just on the table. Be sure the candles scattered throughout are properly shaded and placed to avoid fire.

The couple will be supplied for all manner of special occasions with candles chosen from this list:

plain and twisted tapers of varying lengths and diameters
votive style for candle warmers
birthday cake candles
sculptured candles for floating arrangements
candle in demitasse cup
sculptured rose candle in champagne glass
Advent candle for Christmas season
scented decorator candles
anniversary candle to burn each year on their wedding anniversary
bayberry candle in red or green Christmas goblet
zodiac candle
candle holders in various sizes and styles
glass-chimneyed hurricane lamps for single candles
wicks in plastic discs to float alongside flowers
egg-shape candles to rest in aluminum baking cups
fruit or animal shape candles
extra-fat candles to fit into coffee mugs
wax pellets to hold candles on saucers or trays
candle snuffer

Bundle the gifts in a wicker basket or sturdy box that can double for candle storage after it has carried the gifts to the bride and bridegroom.

Book and Record Shower

Honor the happy couple and expand their book and record collections at the same time with a book and record shower.

An evening of dancing or just listening to music is especially appropriate to this theme. Serve mixed drinks, punch or coffee, set out pick-up foods and dips, turn on the record player and have fun.

Decorate with album covers, musical notes, book jackets, concert posters and pages from the music and book sections of your local newspaper.

Be sure to check the couple's current collection before buying books or records, and it won't hurt a bit to come right out and ask if there's a particular favorite they are yearning to own. Or you can put them on their own by having everyone contribute toward a gift certificate from the most completely stocked shop in town.

If you give a book or record by an author or musician who lives in your area, have it autographed. The artist will be flattered and the signature will give an extra flair to your gift.

And here are some accessory ideas that fit into the book and record theme:

BOOKS

bookends
bookmark
bookplates
reading lamp
photo album
bookrack
magazine subscriptions
back rest for reading in bed
budget and financial record book
home medical guide
family legal adviser
game and party books

RECORDS

record cleaner spray
phonograph needle

tape for recorder
record holder
record catalogs

Use the shelves of an empty bookcase or record cabinet to hold the gifts, or file record albums in a wire record holder.

Home Accessories Shower

Chances are the couple's first home will be a furnished apartment, or else they'll start housekeeping with assorted castoffs, hand-me-downs and secondhand pieces. Help them give direction and pizazz to this composite with a home accessories shower.

Invite as many couples as you can to a treasure or scavenger hunt and have a buffet table of snacks, cold drinks and coffee waiting for the hunters at the end of the search. When everyone is back, serve a more substantial meal.

If you know they're in dire need of one special item, such as an occasional table, king-size bedspread or a telephone receiver with punch-digit dialing, chip in as a group for an expensive gift. If they'll be painting walls or refinishing furniture, get a gift certificate they can use for the materials they need.

Otherwise, choose from the finishing touches listed here:

candlesticks
figurines
music box
reading lamp
breakfast-in-bed tray
subscription to a home decorating magazine
magazine rack
bulletin board
magnetic note holders
mug tree
throw rugs
bed pillows
decorator throw pillows
floor cushions
tissue holder

paperweight
piggy bank—toss in a few coins to start them saving for something
    special
short cords for appliances used on counters or tables
sun lamp
world globe
desk susan for clips, pencils and stamps
cigarette box
memo pads
desk barometer
picture frame for their wedding picture
table-top electric fan
fireplace tools
table lighter
door knocker
door chimes
door mat

Stand the packages on a table covered with a paper cloth on which you've pasted house plans clipped from magazines and newspapers.

Home Office Shower

From the start the newlyweds will be faced with paying bills, keeping records and writing letters. Lessen the shock of learning to run the family business by outfitting them with a home office. They'll bless you for years for getting them off to an organized start.

Start with a pancake breakfast, a Scandinavian dinner or evening punch. Then bring in the gifts.

Several guests can chip in for an attaché case to hold papers and records, while others might decide to go together to buy the more expensive machines.

Individual gifts from this list should equip the couple with what they'll need for their first foray into business at home:

small expandable paper file for cancelled checks
letter-size expandable paper file for bills and correspondence
ledger
file folders
letter-size bond, onionskin and carbon paper
envelopes
stamp dispenser
letter opener
ink, pencil and typewriter erasers
stapler
scissors
ruler
paste or glue
cellophane tape
paper clips
compact adding machine
miniature calculator
pencil sharpener
personal phone directory
memo pads
pens
pencils
stationery
address book
stamps
return address stamp or labels

If you can at least partly empty your desk, place the gifts on top of it and in the drawers. Or place them in a sturdy storage box, perhaps one of the brightly colored ones sold in stationery stores, with an inventory of the donors atop the pile.

Kitchen Shower

To make their kitchen the heart of their first home, be sure the couple has all the necessary and at least some of the extra cooking equipment.

What you give will be determined by what they already own. Many of today's singles have at least a start on kitchen essentials if either has had a bachelor pad, if there have been other kitchen showers or if the bride has been of a practical bent in assembling her hope chest.

Check to see what, if anything, they have accumulated. If they're starting from scratch, circulate a list of basic equipment to those on the guest list, asking them to choose from the essentials. If they already have some things, concentrate on the interesting gadgets that make cooking more fun.

Plan the whole party around the kitchen theme. Spread a buffet breakfast or dinner on the kitchen counter if possible and use mixing bowls, pans, measuring cups, canisters and cookie jars as serving dishes. Arrange a centerpiece of radishes, carrots, beets and parsley in a footed colander, or make a bouquet of small kitchen tools which can go to the bride.

Here are categorized gift suggestions. Take your pick from:

GROUP GIFTS

electric blender
broiler-rotisserie—one that can also bake is even better
electric coffee makers—family and party sizes
electric coffee mill
small electric brewer—for soup, instant beverages or to cook an
    egg or two
espresso coffee maker
countertop electric mixer with accessories and extra beaters
electric skillet—if it's Teflon-lined, add a clutch of special cooking
    tools
deep fat cooker
electric casserole
electric roaster
warming tray
automatic can opener
electric knife sharpener
electric griddle
combination waffle iron and sandwich grill
electric knife
automatic toaster or toaster-oven
portable mixer with extra beaters

electric juicer
electric ice crusher
set of kitchen cabinet organizers and undercabinet kitchen drawers
ice cube bin to fit in freezer section of refrigerator
fanciful kitchen clock

KITCHEN BASICS

pint- and quart-size saucepans with lids
3-quart double boiler
6- and 10-inch skillets
5-quart Dutch oven
trio of nested mixing bowls
large flat roasting pan
meat loaf-size roasting pan
2 (8-inch) square cake pans and racks
2 cookie sheets
9-inch round pie plate
rolling pin
largish colander
tea strainer
sieve
metal tongs
meat thermometer
paring, chopping, butcher and serrated slicing knives
potato peeler
cooking fork
slotted cooking spoon
2 spatulas—1 narrow, 1 wider turner
rotary egg beater
salad fork and spoon
manual can and jar openers
2-cup glass measuring cup
potato masher
set of measuring spoons
flour sifter
1- and 2-quart casseroles
small vegetable brush
grater

6- and 12-cup muffin tins
canister set
butter or sauce brush
kitchen shears
rubber scrapers
pot holders
sponges
dishcloths
kitchen towels
aprons—his and hers
nylon scrubber
pre-soaped scouring pads

GADGETS AND EXTRAS

egg slicer
teakettle
pepper mill
funnel
apple slicer-corer
food chopper
garlic press
wooden cutting board
meatball shaper
melon baller
cheese slicer
poultry shears
large and small wire whisks
collapsible vegetable steamer
giant eyedropper basting tool
ladle
vari-shaped wooden cooking spoons
ice cream scoop
lemon grater
tiny pot for melting butter
butter cube cutter
timer
gelatin molds
oven, candy and meat thermometers

folding stepladder
cake decorating kit
cookie press
cookie cutters
asparagus steamer
fish broiler
soufflé dish
non-stick omelet pan
mini-size baking pans
wire lettuce drainer
fruit bowl or basket
lattice pie crust cutter
ice bucket and tongs
mortar and pestle
carved pastry roller
set of individual casseroles
bread basket
pots of chives, mint, herbs
egg separator
hamburger press
wall-hanging racks for pans
   and kitchen tools
spice rack

Present the gifts in a step-on garbage can, in plastic storage bins or piled on a kitchen table.

Pantry or Staple Shower

So they won't wipe out the first two weeks' food budget just stocking those yawning kitchen cupboards, shower the about-to-be-marrieds with basic non-perishable food items. Invite a crowd and you'll save money for the guests, too. None of these items is expensive in itself, it's only the totals that are staggering.

Plan the party as well as the gifts around food: a potluck buffet, a Sunday brunch or evening get-together with drinks and a sandwich buffet.

A note of caution: Do *not* take the labels off the cans. Far from being funny, it might prove the last straw to the nervous young cook to be faced with a shining array of cans, the contents of which she hasn't the faintest inkling.

Among the staples the guests contribute should be:

granulated, lump, brown and powdered sugar
salt and pepper
flour
baking powder
baking soda
coffee, tea and cocoa
dried herbs and spices
canned goods of all kinds
vinegar
dehydrated soups
cooking sherry
packaged Holland Rusk or melba toast
canned meats
catsup and mustard
pickles, olives and bottled relishes
cooking oil
shortening
cornstarch

And don't neglect the non-food staples, such as:

paper towels and napkins
cellophane wrap
aluminum foil
sandwich bags
shelf paper
scouring pads and scrubbers
soap holder

Request fancy gift wraps as a counterpoint to the serviceability of the gifts, and stuff them into a borrowed grocery cart topped with a pegged grocery shopping memo, printed check lists or a kitchen slate with the gift items checked off or noted.

Gourmet Shower

At the other end of the spectrum are the gourmet foods which might overextend the couple's food budget but are still things they'd enjoy having on hand.

Choose from non-perishable jars and tins of:

savory cocktail food—Tom Thumb size corn on the cob, miniature pickled green tomatoes, marinated mushrooms
almond and anchovy paste
canned pâté
caviar
canapé spreads
special jams, syrups and honey
wine and herb vinegars
Italian, Greek or Spanish olive oil
imported litchi and macadamia nuts
imported cookies
truffles
saffron
artichoke hearts
wild rice
pickled peppers
chutney
imported cheeses

smoked oysters
imported teas
special coffee blends
brandied peaches or apricots
marinade sauce
vanilla beans
sweet pickled watermelon
sunflower seeds
anchovy fillets
kippered herring
grinder for whole spices

Pack the gifts into shopping bags decorated with foreign language food phrases or with labels from gourmet food containers.

POUND SHOWER

Combine the best of staple and gourmet worlds by giving a shower of foods that are sold by the pound. Choose gifts in pound lots from the suggestions above and bag them in giant grocery sacks.

Emergency Shelf

Into each marriage unexpected dinner guests arrive. Lessen the shock for the bride by giving an Emergency Shelf shower. Each guest brings the recipe for a favorite dish that can be concocted from ingredients kept on hand just for that purpose. It's also a nice idea to give the bride the non-perishable basis for the recipe or a special tool, utensil or pan needed to prepare it.

Since recipes bore most men to death, this had best be an all girl party with an especially frilly refreshment table. Use a wedding ring theme in decorations: cut ring-shaped hoops from gold and silver paper and twine with artificial orange blossoms or other bridal flowers.

Keep the ring theme in the refreshments: sandwiches cut with a round cutter, ring mold salad, doughnuts and ring-shaped cookies.

Tape the recipe cards on satin ribbons and hang from a large gold-painted ring or hoop.

Spice Shower

Spices mean creativity in cooking and are a good shower theme.

Choose a party that has out-of-the-ordinary food—an evening of "Love Everybody" punch, a tasting session or a late night supper—and invite as many people as you can.

Request dress-up clothes and feature flowers in your decorations. Remember that a profusion of greens makes a relatively modest number of flowers seem positively lavish, so use them freely throughout the party area.

Most of the gifts for this shower are inexpensive enough for individuals to give, though there may be some collaboration on cookbooks.

The supermarket spice section is only the basic source of gifts for a Spice Shower. In addition to the bottles and jars of spices found there, suggest the following:

empty containers for the honorées to fill themselves
spice bottle labels
grinders for whole spices
spice and herb specialty cookbooks
wooden counter racks for constantly used spices
metal cabinet door racks for extras and seldom used spices
what-to-use-with-what spice chart
dish towels decorated with spice jars
small pots of seeds for starting a herb garden

Present the gifts in a cardboard or wooden box stenciled with the names of spices and herbs or labels from spice jars. It will double nicely as a container in which to carry home the loot.

Can Shower

Put an end to the stale jokes about brides and cans by showing the couple just how endless and exciting the list of things you can buy in cans has become.

Make this an informal party and use cans as part of the décor. Drip hot wax on tin can lids for candle holders, arrange flowers in tall cans and use the smaller, wider tins to serve nuts and candy. Serve canned or bottled food (ham, baked beans, fruits) from the original containers and use baby food cans for cigarettes or small bouquets.

The fanciest electric can opener you can find makes a marvelous group gift, but your guests will probably have more fun seeing how many different things they can discover that are put up in cans. In some areas you can even have the department store "can" your gift in the wildest-ever gift tins.

Ignore the obvious canned staples for some of these:

cocktails (a double Martini with enough for a dividend)
canned ice
sturdy hand can opener
aerosol cleaners
canned heat for chafing dish or fondue pot
push-button fire extinguisher
Run Stop stocking spray
spray starch
hair spray
spray paint

Pack the gifts in cardboard containers salvaged from the grocery store.

Bottle or Jar Shower

Just as challenging for the gift selector is the bottle or jar shower and the results will be equally pleasing to the newlyweds.

Again, use the party theme in decorations: candles and flowers in jars, apothecary jars for nuts and nibbles, condiments in their own bottles or jars and baby food jars to hold cigarettes and kitchen matches.

The gifts, which can range from perfume to pickles, should include:

cocktail mixes
hot buttered rum or Tom and Jerry batter
wines and liquors
watermelon rind pickles
mint or cinnamon pears

olive oil
orange blossom honey
paste or glue
hand lotion or cream
shaving lotion
cologne

Pack the gifts in bottle cartons or a wicker storage basket.

Breakfast Shower

Enable the bridal couple to start the day right via a breakfast shower of things they'll need for cooking and serving breakfast.

Sunday brunch is a great setting for this party. Give yourself a chance to shine by whipping up something especially delicious for a buffet breakfast. Make the party elegant with heaps of flowers in your loveliest containers, a handsome cloth and serve with your best silver and china.

If there's a special appliance they need, give it as a group gift. If they're all set in that department, ask the guests to scour the gadget counters for the cleverest gimmicks they can unearth.

GROUP GIFTS

electric frypan	electric hand mixer
electric griddle	electric coffee maker
waffle maker	electric juicer
automatic toaster	set of breakfast china
blender	

GADGET GIFTS

grapefruit spoons	butter dish
egg timer	jam jar
pair of eggcups	syrup pitcher
tea ball	whisk
butter paddles	egg poacher
melon baller	pair of place mats and napkins
egg turner	fruit dishes
wooden mixing spoon	eggbeater

serrated slicing knife   pot holders
grapefruit knife   egg scissors for cutting boiled eggs
juice squeezer

BREAKFAST RECIPES PLUS

Ask each guest to bring her favorite recipe for a special breakfast treat, plus a utensil necessary for preparing it. If the male guests aren't heavy on culinary skills, tell them to choose the tastiest looking mix on the grocery shelf and to add the pan or baking dish needed to prepare it.

Some other ideas:

blueberry muffins—with a muffin tin
waffles—with a mixing bowl
homemade syrup—with a serving pitcher
eggs Benedict—with a wire whisk for the sauce
coffee cake—with baking pan
omelet—with a turner or special omelet pan
popovers—with a mixing spoon
step-by-step directions for making coffee—with sugar and cream
    servers
step-by-step directions for making tea—with a teapot

Pack the gifts in a market basket.

Buffet Recipes Plus

Get help preparing the party food and add to the bride's recipe collection at the same time with a buffet dinner and recipe shower.

To avoid duplications, plan the menu yourself. Ask guests to bring their specialties and the recipes written on 3 × 5-inch cards. Unattached men can bring relishes, sugar, cream and butter, plus the appropriate serving dish, spoon or fork. Your job is to get everything set up, and make and serve the coffee.

The menu should include:

hors d'oeuvres
several casseroles with meat, seafood, egg or cheese bases
potatoes
vegetables

27

molded salad
vegetable salad
fruit salad
hot breads
butter, jam and jelly
relishes
dessert
coffee

Make the gift presentation simple: an indexed recipe box with the new recipes filed therein and the serving dishes and utensils on a utility tray.

Picnic or Barbecue Shower

Most couples like to eat outdoors, at least occasionally, and will welcome a collection of useful picnic or barbecue accessories.

Key the party to the shower theme by having a picnic or cookout at the beach, in the park or in your own backyard. If it's not the picnic season, bring the outdoors in and set up the party on the dining room table or in the middle of the living room floor. Check the section on individual parties for some outdoor entertaining ideas to supplement your own standbys.

If the couple is really big for cookouts, suggest a barbecue grill, Coleman stove, ice cream freezer or outdoor games as chip-in gifts. Others can choose from these less expensive items:

plastic or sturdy paper plates and cups
basket-type paper plate holders
large paper napkins
straws
stainless steel eating utensils
serving spoons
plastic or terrycloth tablecloth
covered plastic food containers

spillproof salt and pepper shakers
sugar and powdered cream containers
candle holders with hurricane globes
patio torch
paper towels
rolls of waxed paper, plastic wrap and aluminum foil
cutting board or block
sharp knife
styrofoam cold chest
large size vacuum bottle
can and bottle opener
cotton blanket
folding cook grill
long-handled sandwich toaster
long-handled barbecue tools
skewers or kebobs
asbestos-lined cooking mitts
charcoal briquets
electric fire starter
fire starter fluid
kitchen matches in waterproof container
fire tongs and rake
huge chef's apron for each
plastic-lined zippered container for non-perishable condiments
insulated cool-pack
tins of "canned" ice
plastic garbage bags
heavy-duty scraper for cleaning grill
insect repellent
first aid kit
sponge or disposable towels
plastic food bags

Gather the gifts into a large picnic basket or sturdy wooden box that can double later as a carrier.

Cookbook Shower

Does the bride's cooking prowess, or lack of it, doom her hapless mate to an unimaginative diet of frozen dinners and packaged mixes?

You can save the day for both of them with a shower of cookbooks.

Emphasize good cooking in the party food by serving a planned buffet for which each guest prepares a dish which is his or her particular specialty. Use cooking utensils in the decorations: a coffee-pot to hold flowers, fresh fruits or vegetables heaped into a colander, terry kitchen towels as place mats, hot-dish holders as trivets and napkins of kitchen toweling.

Collect a set sum from each guest in advance and designate the most creative cook in the crowd to choose the gifts. Given a chance, most men like to shine in the kitchen, so caution the shopper to keep the bridegroom in mind as she's scanning cookbook titles.

After checking to see what volumes the couple already owns, select cookbooks from the suggested classifications. Since new cookbooks come out constantly, no specific titles are suggested.

an all-inclusive basic text
collection based on canned and convenience foods—Don't laugh.
   It's handy when the bride is in a hurry!
menus and recipes for two
various ethnic collections
budget cookery
"after five" quick cookery
personal recipe book
desserts
freezer recipes
blender cookbook
party plans and recipes
gourmet cookbook

Use a countertop book rack to hold the individually wrapped volumes.

Fix-It Shower

Take pity on the not necessarily handy man—and his new wife—who soon will be faced with perplexing home maintenance chores by showering them with implements for making minor repairs around the house.

Make this an informal party, perhaps a progressive dinner with the gifts waiting at the last house on the tour.

Several guests can band together for some of the more expensive items, such as a reference encyclopedia of home repairs or small power tools. For the rest, a walk through the hardware store will yield a spate of useful gifts, including:

claw hammer
small screwdriver with several interchangeable shafts
hand saw
machine oil
sandpaper
electrician's and adhesive tape
masking tape
adjustable wrench
sewing machine tune-up kit
drills and discs for power tools
folding carpenter's rule
retracting tape measure
heavy duty stapler
pliers
wrench
chisel
assortment of nails
roll of electric cord
extra lamp and appliance plugs
extra light fuses
small stepladder
all-purpose glue
work scissors
basket or box to store and carry tools

Hang small packages on a peg board, à la home workshop, with larger ones lodged at the base. Or stack them on a worktable made of planks stretched across small tables or wooden sawhorses borrowed from a lumber yard or hardware store.

Uglies Shower

Housework isn't a bit glamorous, but it does have to be done. So even the happiest bride and groom need the "uglies," the props for making tedious cleaning chores more bearable.

Contrast the utility of the shower theme with the zingiest party possible, perhaps drinks and dancing with a posh late night supper.

Make a table centerpiece of doll-size laundry baskets filled with flowers and surrounded by other toy cleaning equipment.

If a fond parent or in-law or doting grandmother wants to supply a special gift, suggest a vacuum cleaner or electric sweeper. The rest of the less impressive but equally necessary cleaning items can be supplied by the couple's friends:

scouring powder
johnny mop
dustcloths
soap-filled scrubbing pads
sponges
nylon net scrubber
cloth-paper towels
broom
dustpan
dust mop
sponge mop
Venetian blind duster
furniture polish
spray-can dusting and polishing agents
liquid mirror cleaner
silver polish
spot remover
oven cleaner
laundry hamper
large plastic pail
scrub brush
toilet bowl cleaner
floor-washing powders and liquids
floor wax for both wood and linoleum
wax applicator
rubber gloves for wet work
cotton gloves for dusting and polishing
disposable plastic work gloves
garbage can

lidded kitchen trash container
plastic or oiled paper garbage sacks
wastebasket
paper towels
spray window cleaners
ammonia
window squeegee
plastic dishpan
dish drainer
car wax
metal polish
trash burner
book on how to clean house
tote tray or basket for carrying small cleaning aids

Bundle the small packages into a handled basket that can be used later to carry cleaning supplies from room to room. Dump the others into a huge soap carton from the grocery store or a plastic scrub pail or wastebasket.

Garden Shower

Green thumbs don't always just happen. Sometimes they're cultivated through necessity. If the about-to-be-weds will be living in a house, if their apartment has a patio or balcony or even if they've no outdoor space to call their own, they can still grow plants, so don't discount the importance of a garden shower.

Serve breakfast, cocktails or dinner outdoors, in a real garden if you can. But if it's winter or you have no yard, decorate as though it were outdoors with garden furniture, masses of flowers and greenery, a centerpiece of small potted plants (give them to the honor guests), even a chicken-wire trellis entwined with paper flowers or a low white "picket" fence cut from cardboard.

If the couple has little or no actual ground space now, give them house plants, gardening books and magazine subscriptions. If they're digging in the dirt from the beginning, a group gift of a wheelbarrow or lawn mower will be most welcome. For individual gifts, choose:

spade
rake
weeder
hoe
trowel
clippers
pruning tools
packets of seeds
bulbs
seedlings in dirt-filled boxes
cuttings from your own plants
house plants
shrubs
peat moss
fertilizer
special plant foods
weed killer
planters of various sizes and shapes
flower tubs
garden hose
sprinkler head
patio lamp
lawn furniture
garden hat
gardening gloves
promise of help in weeding, watering and other chores
measuring cups and spoons for plant food
garden catalogs
gardening pamphlets from government agencies
Farmer's Almanac
soil-testing kit
liniment
suntan lotion

weatherproof plant tags
kneeling mat

Trundle in a gift-packed wheelbarrow, with smaller presents tucked into a giant sprinkler can or a wooden box which can hold hand tools and other garden gear later.

Closet Shower

Chances are there won't be nearly enough closet space in the honeymoon abode, but friends can help minimize the crowding with a closet shower of coordinated storage items.

Make your party different by celebrating a special or offbeat holiday or by choosing foreign food and decorations.

It's best to collect in advance from the guests and delegate the shopping so all items will match. Be sure to check the bride's bedroom color scheme before selecting the gifts. Also check on the kind of closet doors they'll have before deciding on door-hanging items.

Hope you don't run out of money before you gather up these indispensables:

garment bags
hatbox
wooden suit hangers
padded satin dress hangers
skirt, blouse and slacks hangers
shoe trees
compartmented shoe and handbag holders
floor or wall shoe racks
see-through plastic storage boxes in several sizes
adjustable shelves, pole and brackets kit
cardboard suitcase storage box
tie and ribbon racks
porcelain or metal hooks
shelf paper
cedar spray
perfumed spray mist
pomander ball or pull-wick air freshener
door-hung, flip-down dressing table unit

full-length door mirror
compartmented bag for odds and ends
plastic boot bin

If you can, borrow a portable paperboard closet or storage unit and put the gifts in it. Otherwise, place the beautifully wrapped packages on a card table or serving cart.

Bathroom Shower

Spark up the couple's bathroom décor with special small delights, organizers and accessories.

For decorating and serving use a heap of colorful guest soaps in a wicker basket for a centerpiece, solid-color terrycloth hand towels for place mats and coordinating print washcloths for napkins.

For group gifts consider "his and hers" electric shavers, a facial sauna, electric toothbrush, whirlpool tub attachment or piles of the best-looking towel sets you can find.

On their own, but keeping in mind the bride's avowed color scheme, guests may choose from:

brass, aluminum or wooden towel "tree"
wall cabinet for bottles and jars
a plant that needs lots of moisture in a wall-hanging planter
hanging or standing bathroom shelves
bath, hand and guest soaps
soap dish
toothbrushes
toothpaste, mouthwash and dental floss
key-type squeezer that gets out the last bit of toothpaste
plastic-lined fabric shower curtain
matching window curtains
fabric lid and tank covers
bath mat
shower caddy for shampoo and soap
aluminum door hooks .
makeup mirror with regular and magnifying sides
bathroom scale
tilt-bin tube organizer for medicine chest shelf

inflatable bath pillow
plastic tub tray for book and grooming implements
decorative jars and bottles
tissue box cover
bath salts and oils, bubble bath and shower gelée
dusting powder and after-bath lotion
pre- and after-shave lotions, shave cream
toilet and facial tissues
retractable clothesline or hanging rack for hand laundry
aerosol air freshener
tile, floor and bowl-cleaning preparations
johnny mop and refills

Group the gifts in and around a straw, wicker or plastic bathroom hamper.

Laundry Shower

Whether they have their own appliances or use the laundromat, washday will be a part of married life, so prepare the couple for laundry duty with the items they'll need for keeping clean.

Since this, too, is a "practical" party, be zany in your planning by accenting fun, food and good cheer with a cocktail or coffee-tasting party.

Use the laundry theme in table decorations by filling mini-laundry baskets from the toy department with flowers and fruit. Fill out the centerpiece with other doll-size laundry equipment.

While most of the suggested gifts are inexpensive, several might want to combine forces to buy a steam-dry iron or a fancy adjustable ironing board. Others can provide:

washing powder
pre-soak solution
liquid and powder bleach
soap flakes
liquid detergent
water softener
cold water soap
special washing preparation for permanent press fabrics

stain remover
bluing
regular and spray starch
palm-size plastic scrubbing board for hand washing
wooden clothespins in hanging holder
plastic hangers and clips for drip-dry fabrics
sweater dryer
posy-sprinkled ironing board cover
hot iron stand
iron cord holder
sprinkling bottle
plastic bag for storing dampened clothes
pressing cloth
steam iron boot for shine-free pressing
sleeve board
pressing mitt

Wheel in the gifts in a canvas clothes sorter, or put them in a huge laundry basket.

Box or Basket Shower

Where to store things is a major problem for most newlyweds. While there's no easy solution, a box or basket shower will help them keep some of the clutter out of sight.

Serve a Sunday lunch or late evening supper packed in individual boxes and use baskets as containers for fruit, snacks and matches.

Several persons can be asked to bring two or three basket holders to keep paper plates steady (combined, they will make a set), while some of the others can chip in to buy a fitted picnic basket or a bathroom hamper.

One bit of advice: don't fill the boxes or baskets. The object of the shower is to give containers to hold the paraphernalia they can't store otherwise.

BOXES

stamp	makeup
stationery	jewelry—one for each of them
pencil	hosiery

bread	hat
cake	firewood
pie	tool
candy	window
cigarette	blanket
kitchen match	metal storage box with lock
recipe	refrigerator
handkerchief	gift certificate for bank safe-deposit rental

BASKETS

sewing
market
serving baskets for baking dishes
wicker mail organizer
fruit
waste
laundry
styrofoam-lined basket ice bucket
serving bowl holder
flowerpot holder
bread
cracker
snack server
rattan trivets and hot mats
woven napkin rings
bun server with warmer-liner
basketweave mirror frame
woven spice holder
wicker tissue holder
hanging flower basket

Use a wicker bathroom hamper, plastic laundry basket or huge paper box to hold the gifts.

Plastic Shower

Help that great modern innovation, plastic, get the newlyweds off to an organized housekeeping start.

Invite as many people as you can so the honorés will get maximum advantage from the vast range of plastic items available these days. Make it comfortable: a Gay Nineties theme with beer, food, harmonizing and fun.

A welcome group gift is a set of melamine dinnerware, but your guests will probably agree that it's more fun to choose individual gifts for this party. Tell them to search hardware stores, housewares departments, even drugstores and cosmetic counters, to turn up these plastic gifts:

apron
covered refrigerator dishes
spatulas
mixing bowls
bags in various sizes
see-through kitchen wrap
pitchers
breadbox
covered cake storer
covered pie carrier
dishpan
dustpan
pail
picnic plates and cups
table place mats
coasters
paper napkin holder
garment bags
mending box
shower curtain
bathroom glass
wastebasket
soap dish
appliance covers
curler caddy
cosmetic bag
drip-dry hangers
lint brush

shampoo scrubber
nailbrush
cellophane tape dispenser
desk lamp
light switch cover
flower container

Present the gifts in a swing-top plastic kitchen trash basket or the largest plastic basket you can find.

Brush Shower

At first glance a "brush off" doesn't seem complimentary to the newlyweds, but a shower of brushes will be useful to them.

Have a dessert party, with either a choice of luscious pastries or a single cake large enough to serve everyone and decorated in a wedding design.

Keep the table decorations simple, with a centerpiece of flowers or fruit and belie the practicality of the shower gifts by requesting sumptuous wrapping.

An electric toothbrush is an appropriate group gift, or simply turn the guests loose to see what they can turn up, such as:

pair of shaving brushes—a regular one for him, a tiny size for her
bath brush
scrub brush
hairbrush for each
vegetable brush
nailbrush
barbecue or pastry brush
whisk broom
clothesbrush
brush cleaner
pet brush—if they have a dog or cat
brush hair rollers
makeup brushes
lint remover

Heap the packages into a fake wedding cake or an enormous gift box papered with bridal wrappings.

Soap Shower

From utter luxury to strictly practical, soap looms large in everyday living, so the couple will need the whole spectrum of soaps they'll get at a soap shower.

To contrast the serviceability of the gifts, plan a plush evening punch party and decorate with masses of flowers in your fanciest containers.

Intensely practical shoppers will choose the unadorned necessities, but urge that the fancier items also find their way to the party. Have your guests choose from:

unscented bath and hand soaps
perfumed bars of various sizes in both men's and women's scents
liquid face cleanser
shaving soap
bubble bath
shower soap on a rope
guest soaps in various sizes and shapes
laundry soaps
pre-soak compounds
bleach
dishwashing detergent
sculptured soap flowers
floor-cleaning powders and liquids
cold water soap
soap dishes and holders
window cleaner
soap-measuring scoop
scouring powder

Stuff the packages into a laundry bag, supersize grocery sacks or a string shopping bag.

Cutlery Shower

Even the couple that theoretically "has everything" doesn't usually have all of the cutlery found on today's market. Cut through to the heart of things by giving them a shower to fill in their cutlery supplies.

Invite your guests to a buffet supper or other evening party or, if you prefer, a Sunday coffee or brunch. Include as many people as you can so you can outfit the couple as completely as possible.

Place knives or butter spreaders in their silver pattern, electric shears, a carving set, an electric knife sharpener, steak knives or an electric carving knife are good gifts for more than a single donor. Or they can choose individual presents from these:

paring knife	kitchen shears
butter knife	straight utility scissors
fruit knife	pinking shears
spreader	bent shears
French chef's knife	cuticle scissors
butcher knife	barber shears
bread knife	straight or safety razor
ham slicer	blunt pocket scissors
sandwich knife	thread clipper
utility knife	embroidery scissors
roast slicer	nail clipper
peeler	can opener
cheese knife	hand knife sharpener
cake breaker	knife rack
pie server	

If you can get hold of a mammoth pair of wooden scissors (the kind they use to cut ceremonial ribbons) or can make some of heavy cardboard, suspend the smaller packages from them. Or insert knives in a knife rack and place the other gifts in plastic kitchen drawer dividers. Or just pile the gifts into a utility basket.

Paper Shower

Take advantage of the paper-mania which is sweeping the country and make married life easier by gifting the bridal couple with an assortment of the bright, beautiful and inexpensive "throwaways" designers are turning out in all sorts of up-to-the-minute colors and styles.

While that old paper standby, money, is always welcome, there are all sorts of other paper basics—from bikinis to easy chairs—being turned out these days. They're sturdy and high-styled, a far cry from the plain paper napkins your mother deplored.

It's fun to set the mood by sending a paper dress to each gal with her party invitation. Decorate with paper flowers, serve on paper plates and use paper as much as possible in the other decorations: swathes of crepe paper around the table edge, paper streamers across the ceiling and paper posters on the walls.

As hostess, suggest that whenever the guests choose gifts that have been treated with a fire-resistant finish they look for water repellent and abrasion-resistant treatment as well.

It's a good idea to add some advice to the honor guests: While some throwaways can be laundered, washing removes most fire-retarding finishes. If there are no ironing instructions, iron with a cool iron. Keep paper clothing on a hanger, not in a drawer. Wipe paper furniture clean with a damp cloth.

What to give? Choose from these varied possibilities:

bedspread
window curtains
draperies
sheets
pillowcases
blankets
liners for sleeping bags
matching plates, cups, napkins, coasters and tablecloths
dishcloths

guest and kitchen towels
aprons
centerpieces
doilies
place mats
papier mâché napkin rings
Japanese lanterns
posters
occasional tables
Tiffany lampshades
stools
storage chests or bins
fiberboard chairs
gift wrap kits
44-inch-wide paper fabric to stitch up as they like
dresses
bikini
sun hat
beach poncho
scuffs
panties
jewelry
belt
tote bag
playing cards
score pads
matches
facial and toilet tissue
recipe cards
stationery
paperback books
paint buckets
fold-up paper wig stand
personalized postal cards
message pads
shelf paper
grocery checklist forms
mailing labels

waxed paper
address book

Staple gift-holding bags together out of heavy duty foil or wrapping paper.

Miscellaneous Shower

The only time a miscellaneous shower is really fun is when it's for couples. Ask the gals to bring a gift for the bride, the men for the bridegroom. Or, for maximum hilarity, reverse the order.

Go all out for this party by tossing a Hawaiian luau. Be sure to specify informal, Hawaiian style dress and decorate lavishly in a tropical mood.

As for the gifts, ingenuity counts here, but nothing really personal, please!

FOR HER

purse organizer
wiglet
wig stand
pill box
long-handled bath brush
locket with his picture in it
two-way hand mirror
slant board for exercising
eye shadow pallette
trio of lipsticks
flower-studded checkbook cover
"washing machine" for contact lenses
credit card holder
table-top wooden spectacles holder
return address labels with her new name

FOR HIM

hand size steamer for pressing trouser creases
monogrammed golf balls
zippered carryall for car visor

paisley formal dress cummerbund
travel kit
combination tissue dispenser-litter container for the car
hand warmer for outdoorsmen
doorway chinning bar
cigarette lighter
tartan plaid checkbook cover
shoeshine kit

Bring out the gifts in two oversize plastic wastebaskets, each neatly monogrammed with one of the couple's initials.

Hobby Shower

If the couple shares a hobby, or even if they have separate avocations, use their leisure time interests as the basis for a shower.

Tools, equipment, gadgets, supplies and accessories for artists, fishermen, hunters, sculptors, bird watchers, skiers, sailors, readers, golfers or hikers are fun to choose and welcomed by the honor guests. If you're unsure of their needs, a gift certificate is always a good idea.

If the bridegroom is a sportsman but his new wife is a neophyte, try giving her something connected with his hobby so she can at least make a stab at joining him. If these are funny, so much the better: a suit of flowered long thermal underwear for the new gal skier; a pair of hip-high wading boots, an electric worm getter or a lure maker for the fisherman's bride; goggles or lip pomade for the newcomer to the ski slopes; bowling shoes for the beginning bowler, or iridescent golf balls for the golfer-to-be.

Pack gifts for this shower in a fisherman's creel, ski tote, bowling bag or other appropriate container.

Honeymoon Shower

Say bon voyage to the honeymooners with a miscellany of travel accessories to take on their wedding trip.

Collect as large a crowd as possible for an Around the World or other party featuring foreign food, and fit the decorations either to their way of traveling or point of destination. Incorporate toy trains, cars, airplanes or boats into the table decorations. Use maps, travel

47

posters and timetables for wall hangings, and play records of regional music of the area they'll visit as background for the party.

Don't get a group gift for this shower. It's more fun to make up a collection of trinkets that are worth their weight in helpfulness. If they're traveling by car, also investigate the gift suggestions in the "Moving Away" party plan.

However and wherever they travel, these will come in handy:

guidebooks
camera film
writing kit and ballpoint pen
"fresh up" kit for each with toothbrush and paste, pill box and
    collapsible cup
folding plastic hangers
travel slippers for each
laundry kit with line, clips and packets of detergent
travel iron
disposable shoeshine packets
compressed washcloths
travel diary
sewing kit
first aid kit
small flashlight
travel thermos
travel alarm clock
foldup paper wig stand
pocket-size packets of facial tissues
flat stopper—in case washbasin doesn't have one
sun lotion
lip pomade
pre-moistened towelettes
stain remover packets
combination can-bottle opener
aspirin and antacid pills
laxative and its opposite
collapsible wheel and strap contraption for pulling luggage
folding plastic raincoat apiece
terry shoe bags

plastic-lined makeup kit
deck of cards
baggage tags
small roll transparent tape
jewelry roll
small comb and brush in plastic case for each
hanging travel case with plastic-lined laundry section
nail clippers
nail file
soap dish
shampoo and mouthwash in plastic containers
cold water soap
address book
small clothesbrush
razor blades

If they're traveling to a foreign country, they'll need:

passport case
currency converter
paperback foreign language phrase books
foreign currency—your bank can get it for you
letters of introduction to any friends you have in the country
    they're visiting

Pack the packages in a large cardboard carton covered with maps or travel stickers.

Special Time Shower

Enjoy the variety of a miscellaneous shower yet stay within a single theme with a Special Time wedding shower.

Give some of the guests a specific time of day and ask them to bring a gift used at that time. Assign a different month to others with instructions to bring a gift appropriate to that time of year.

Cover a white paper tablecloth with clock cutouts interspersed with symbols of special holidays and take advantage of the leeway the theme allows to incorporate holiday decorations from Baby New Year to Santa Claus into your party décor.

Skip group gifts for this party to allow your guests free rein to choose the wildest presents they can dream up. If they need a few ideas to spark them, suggest:

cleanup time—broom or dustpan
coffee time—pair of oversize coffee mugs
bath time—long-handled bath brush
vacation time—travel clock
budget time—family expense ledger
mealtime—table accessories
fun time—pair of movie tickets
work time—dish towels for her, hammer for him
party time—frilly apron
nap time—eyeshade or coverlet
travel time—cosmetic bag for her, shaving gear kit for him
cocktail time—small Martini pitcher or two cocktail glasses
January—adjustable calendar
February—heart-shape cake pan or canned and packaged ingredients for a cherry pie
March—rabbit's foot to protect against the Ides of March
April—guide for preparing Income Tax return
May—May basket with flower seeds or flower-sprinkled pillowcases
June—wedding bell gelatin mold
July—an American flag
August—small suitcase for vacation
September—rake for gathering fall leaves
October—Halloween cookie cutters
November—canned pumpkin and sweet potatoes for Thanksgiving dinner
December—glossy Christmas tree ornament

A cardboard carton papered with calendar sheets and pages from a date book or appointment memo will double for presenting the gifts and carrying them home after the party.

Christmas Shower

Basic Christmas decorations represent a healthy investment for a young couple. If they've had a number of more conventional showers they, and the guests, will surely welcome the change of pace a Christmas Shower brings.

Unless the party is given in winter, finding gifts may be a challenge, so issue invitations in plenty of time for searchers to turn up Christmas treasures. Those who can handcraft items will have an easier time of it, because they can make their gifts. But catalogs, import shops and helpful department store clerks can help the others.

If yours is a December party, invite everyone to a tree-trimming party. But even if the party falls outside the Yule season keep Christmas in mind when decorating and planning refreshments. Colored lights, tinsel, artificial holly, Christmas cakes and cookies, punch, fruitcake and similar food and decorations can be used any time of the year to add a different air to the party.

Instead of a group gift, ask each guest to do his own Christmas shopping for:

tree lights
ornaments
tinsel
tree stand
foil icicles
doorknob hangers
Christmas candles
Advent calendar
start a Christmas Club account
door wreath
Christmas gift wrapping paper
holly printed paper baking cups
Christmas print paper napkins and coasters
metal tray with Christmas motif
candy canes
greeting card display tree
Christmas card and list file
Christmas greeting cards
ceramic Santa candle holders

Stash the gifts in a white cloth Santa's pack or in a cardboard carton covered with brick fireplace paper or Christmas gift wrap.

3
Wedding Showers–
All Girl

Showers have traditionally been all girl affairs and, in some cases, it's still the best idea.

Parties asking for purely feminine gifts are best left to the ladies. They'll be free to enjoy the gift opening, and the hostess can be frillier in her decorations and refreshments than if there are males present.

So if you choose one of the parties in this section, go all out for femininity, frivolity and the kind of fun possible only when the gals get together.

Trousseau Accessories Shower

While the bride will probably want to choose her own lingerie for her trousseau, her friends can enjoy the fun of helping her by giving her some of the extra, feminine accessories every girl craves.

If it's an afternoon party, plan a tea, while an evening shower of this kind calls for punch, fancy sandwiches, even a wedding type cake.

Use a table centerpiece of fresh flowers with your most festive linens, silver and serving pieces.

Small, individual gifts are the order of the day at this party. Be sure to request the daintiest, most elaborate wrappings ever for:

tiny personal laundry bag
curler cap
fancy shower cap big enough to cover rollers
perfumed drawer liner paper
sachet bags and spray
lingerie cases
stocking holder
glove case or box
padded satin clothes hangers
satin pillowcase to protect hairdo
Run Stop stocking spray

Stuff a huge felt stocking with the small packages or store the gifts in a small chest of drawers or miniature hope chest fashioned by papering a covered cardboard container with wood-grained adhesive-backed paper.

Dressing Table Shower

If the bride is lucky enough to have a dressing table of her own, she'll want to receive a stock of accessories for it. Even if she must share the available bathroom space with her new husband, she will still treasure the frilly extras she receives at this party.

The group may want to give a single gift, such as a hair drier, gift certificate for a wig, a set of electric curlers, a facial sauna or a lighted makeup mirror. If you decide instead on individual gifts, be sure to spread the word on the bride's favorite type or brand of scent.

She'll like to have:

perfume
cologne

dusting powder
body lotion
hand cream
hair spray
powder box
wig stand
comb and brush
hair-setting lotion or gel
two-way regular and magnifying mirror
tweezers
nail file
quilted cotton squares
Q-tips
facial tissue
cuticle scissors or nippers
nail polish, base coat, sealer and remover
makeup cape
lipstick caddy
fancy pincushion
tiny mending kit

Arrange the gifts atop a dressing table fashioned by gathering a net skirt on a round table, or deposit them in a pale pink box frilled with white lace.

Linen Shower

Now sleek and chic, linens have moved from their necessary-but-boring classification up front to a page one place in home décor.

Since linen gifts are often costly, you might invite relatives only to a sit down luncheon so the new in-laws can get better acquainted during the party. Or friends of the couple's mothers might want to assume the higher gift cost of adding to the bride's linen trousseau.

If the bride has her heart set on an expensive tablecloth and napkins, a number of guests can buy the cloth and others give her a single napkin each. Or the group may want to splurge on a set of silky sheets and cases with a matching blanket.

You might decide to limit the gifts to napkins only, again with several going together to get sets of cotton or linen luncheon, dinner or cocktail napkins and others contributing packages of smartly styled paper napkins of various sizes. Coordinated towel sets are another treasured group gift.

On the invitation specify what size bed or beds the couple will have, what colors they plan for bedroom, kitchen and bath and the size and kind of dining table they will have. Then suggest:

sheets
pillowcases
pillow covers
mattress pad or cover
blankets
bath, hand and face towels
guest towels
bath mat
tablecloths
place mats
napkins
kitchen towels
dishcloths
beach towels
handkerchiefs

Give the gifts to the bride in a cardboard hope chest or miniature cedar chest or drop the packages into a king size pillow slip.

Silver Accessories Shower

While most gifts of silver fall into the "important wedding gift" category, you can use this traditional bridal theme to lavish silver care items on the bride-elect.

Make this the most elaborate party possible, a garden luncheon, high tea or formal dessert, and use as much silver as you can in decorating: fresh flowers blooming in silver pitchers or bowls, cigarettes in a silver wineglass, candy in a silver vegetable dish or silver gravy boat. And use every bit of silver you can on the table: flatware, water pitcher, serving accessories.

A large tarnish-proof chest for the couple's new flatware is expensive enough to warrant some pooling of resources, but most of the gifts can easily be managed by individuals. If you can't find the storage pouch or bag you want, stitch it up from tarnish-proof cloth, which is sold by the yard, and decorate it with appliqué or the bride's new initials.

The things she'll need to care for her silver properly include:

paste silver polish
hunks of soft flannel or cotton knit cloth for polishing
loosely woven dishcloth for cleaning fork tines
linen towel for buffing
mild liquid detergent or soap for washing
moleskin (manufactured for foot corns) to space on the bottoms or
    feet of silver serving pieces to avoid scratching silver trays
cotton work gloves to wear when polishing (avoid rubber ones
    which cause tarnish)
storage pouches for coffee or teapots and pitchers
smaller pouches for goblets and liqueur glasses
tailored envelopes for trays
storage bags for bowls
polishing mitts to use when dusting silver kept on display

Heap the gifts on a huge silver tray or in a carton covered with aluminum foil. Provide a small silver tray or shallow silver bowl to hold the gift cards as the packages are unwrapped.

Sewing Shower

In her new role as wife, the bride will be faced with some sewing chores, replacing a popped shirt button if nothing else. While nothing except experience will turn a fumbling novice into a competent seamstress, her friends can help the cause with a Sewing Shower.

Gather the gals for morning coffee, then shower the bride with a swarm of sewing basics, gadgets and gimmicks.

If she sews a lot, a group gift of electric shears or a dressmaker's dummy sized to her measurements would be welcome. Otherwise, concentrate on the small necessities:

FOR BEGINNERS

folder of different size needles
thread in basic colors
straight and safety pins
scissors
tape measure
ruler
yardstick
needle threader
card of shirt buttons
snaps, hooks and eyes
pincushion or box
iron-on mending tape
thimble
needle case
hem gauge
skirt marker

IF SHE ALREADY SEWS

subscription to pattern magazine
membership in a fabric club
stitch ripper
zipper adhesive
tracing wheel and paper
dressmaker's "ham" for pressing curved seams
see-through dressmaker's rule
foldaway cutting board
dressmaker's marking pencil
sewing machine needles
extra bobbins
extra-long dressmaker's pins
woven "Made By" labels with her first name
point turner
button gauge
assortment of odd-shape needles for special jobs

Install the gifts in a roomy sewing basket or compartmented sewing box.

KNITTING

If she knits rather than sews, substitute a knitting theme for your party.

Several can go together for a gift certificate for yarn of her choice, but it's more fun to choose gifts from the tools and accessories that abound in knitting departments, such as:

pom pom rings
gauge-check counter
stitch counter
cable stitch counter
cable stitch holders
knitting needle case
tape for counting rows
stitch count markers
knitting needles
crochet hooks
yarn-size sewing needles for stitching finished garments
rubber needle guards to prevent stitches from slipping
small scissors
pattern books

Heap the gifts in a knitting bag or storage box that can be used later to hold extra yarn.

STITCHERY SHOWER

Creative stitchery devotees can also be showered with tools of their trade. Gift certificates for kits or supplies are always a good choice, but individual gifts to supplement her equipment are fun, too. Look for:

adjustable embroidery hoops
embroidery floss in various shades
stamped embroidery work
embroidery needles
transfer patterns

needlepoint patterns
backing for original needlepoint work
yarn-size needles
pattern books.

Use a covered basket or box to hold the gifts at the party, and later the project in progress.

ODDS-AND-ENDS

If the bride is adventurous in trying new handiwork, you might add these to the gift suggestions to start her on a new road:

rug hooks
tatting shuttle
hand loom
crochet hooks
handwork pattern books
"how to" needlecraft books

Give her the gifts in a wood-framed, stand-up handiwork container.

Apron Shower

Giving a shower for the bride who has everything? She'll need aprons, something not considered as a gift possibility often enough.

This is an especially good party to give if lots of the guests sew, as the apron possibilities inherent in a swatch of material and a few bits of trim are fabulous. But seamstresses or not, the guests can find piles of cute aprons in department, variety and specialty stores.

Make this a frivolous party and pull out all the stops in using your nicest china, linens and silver, perhaps for a champagne breakfast. Give some extra thought to flowers to further the femininity.

Group gifts don't work for this type shower. Each guest should search out the most individual apron she can find. It's fun if someone remembers the bridegroom with a man-sized chef's or carpenter's apron.

To equip the bride for every contingency, ask for:

full-length plastic apron for dishwashing
terrycloth half aprons

colorful bib apron for all-purpose duty
frilly cocktail styles for entertaining
half apron with outsize pockets for holding clothespins
gaily printed popovers for maximum coverup
slim smock style for sewing
heavy cotton for outdoor cooking
gardening coverup with pockets for small tools

A lace and heart-trimmed cardboard container will serve beautifully as a gift package holder.

No-Expense Showers

If there have already been several showers given for the bride, don't skip giving another party for her because you think the guests will begin to feel a financial pinch. Just ask for gifts that won't cost anything. Then go all out on refreshments to give the party an especially festive touch.

RECIPE SHOWER

Ask each person to contribute a favorite recipe (concentrate on the easier dishes if she hasn't cooked a lot) written or typed on a 3x5-inch file card and enclosed in a greeting card. If they design their own cards they'll be more personal and more fun. As each card is opened, file the recipe in its proper spot in an indexed recipe file. When the party is over, give the box and recipes to the bride.

IDEA BOOK

Before the party ask each guest to write out a trick for saving time or work or a housekeeping trick she has learned the hard way. Combine them in a looseleaf notebook and present the festively wrapped volume to the guest of honor.

In case some of the guests aren't very ingenious in these matters, here are some hints to keep in reserve:

Unjam a zipper by soaping it.
When you use a spray spot remover that dries to a white powder, use the vacuum cleaner nozzle to take off the dried film.

Keep a napkin holder in the kitchen cabinet to store envelopes of salad dressing, gravy and sauce mixes.

Use an empty six-pack soda carton to carry and store cleaning sprays and bottles.

When frying bacon drain it on a brown paper bag instead of a paper towel—it's just as efficient and a lot cheaper.

Use empty perfume and cologne bottles as lingerie sachets.

A few drops of vanilla on a cotton ball will keep your refrigerator sweet smelling.

GIRL FRIDAY

Each guest pledges a given amount of work for the bride before her first dinner party, a visit from her in-laws or some other special occasion. Make up a schedule with the donor's name, address and phone number and the job she's volunteered to do. Brides will welcome help with:

polishing silver
waxing furniture
pressing table linens
washing "company" china and crystal
cleaning house
arranging flowers
setting the table
making hors d'oeuvres
home hair set and manicure

No-Gift Prenuptial Parties

The perfect way for an adoring grandmother, favorite aunt or an about-to-be in-law to fete the bride is to give a prenuptial party at which no gifts are given.

These frankly female parties are usually more formal than many of the showers, and invitations are sent only to relatives and close friends. Since they are given just before the wedding, careful scheduling is necessary to avoid conflict with other pre-wedding festivities. Check first with the bride and plan as far ahead as you can.

Trousseau Tea

A Trousseau Tea gives the bride a chance to show her new clothes and lingerie to her friends and relatives before she packs for the honeymoon.

Serve a High Tea and provide extra table space to hold the boxes and piles of lingerie and a rack on which to hang dresses, coats, skirts, suits and blouses. Be sure, also, to allow enough time for everyone to peek at all the fripperies before the end of the party.

Gift Display Luncheon

Since the bride will want to share her pleasure in treasured wedding gifts with family and close friends, it is perfectly correct to show her gifts at home. A particularly nice way to do this is to ask intimate female friends and family members of both the bride and bridegroom to come to lunch a few days before the wedding to see the presents.

Since the family dining room has probably been preempted to house the wedding gifts, serve a tray luncheon from the kitchen. Have enough helpers so serving time is cut to the minimum and have someone circulate with coffee, sugar and cream and serve dessert from a side table. Spray-painted cookie sheets topped with lacy paper or linen place mats make handy lap trays.

After lunch, ask the guests to browse through the wedding gifts at their own pace. It is best to display gifts with their gift cards attached in categories of silver, glassware, appliances, linens and miscellaneous items. To save space, show only single place settings of china, flat silver and crystal with all the gift cards from senders of these items. Scatter duplicates and do not place modest gifts next to truly sumptuous ones. Enclose checks in plain white envelopes with the notation "Check from" and the donor's name.

Spinster Dinner

Two or three nights before the wedding, get the bride's wedding attendants and other close friends together for a last gabfest.

Serve a buffet dinner with light dessert, then clear the table for action and let the guests all pitch in to wrap the groom's cake for the wedding reception. This chore goes quickly when everyone helps and conversation can flow uninterrupted as the packets of cake mount.

This is also a good time for the bride to present mementoes of the wedding to the girls in her bridal party.

Bachelor Party

Sponsor a last fling for your brother, nephew or son before he enters matrimony by giving him a bachelor party two or three nights before the wedding. This is often given the same night as the Spinster Dinner, but other than timing there should be no connection between the two. Save this night for men only.

Your part in the undertaking is simple: after consulting the bridegroom on the guest list, issue invitations, arrange for the food and drinks, then *disappear.*

Let the groom decide the tone of the party: perhaps poker or other card games, with plenty to drink and a buffet table loaded with cold meats, cheese, breads of all kinds, condiments, potato chips and dips. Be sure everything can be eaten with the hands so they won't have to cope with plates and silverware. This also makes cleaning up afterward less overwhelming.

Be sure you have plenty of ice, glasses, ashtrays, liquor and mix where the men can get to them easily. Fix more than enough food—chances are they'll eat it all.

During the evening it's traditional to drink a toast (often champagne) to the bride, then shatter the glasses—so they can never be used for a lesser toast. If this is on the agenda, be sure that expendable glasses are provided, there's a safe place to fling them, and the breakage is swept up immediately. The glass-breaking bit is often bypassed at today's bachelor party, as being easier on the glassware, the house and the hostess.

Rehearsal Dinner

An important pre-wedding festivity is the Rehearsal Dinner, which is held the late afternoon or early evening before the wedding, immediately following the wedding rehearsal.

This dinner is usually given by the bridegroom's family, but if this is not practical it may be given by a close relative or old family friend. Things are far too hectic at home for the bride's mother to take on this added chore!

The Rehearsal Dinner is often held at a restaurant or private club, but it can also be a buffet at home.

Both sets of parents, members of the wedding party, the clergyman and his wife are "must" guests. If the budget and space permit, other members of the immediate family, out of town guests and spouses of the wedding attendants may also be included. If you wish, you can invite a few other friends, such as the gal who's been asked to be on hand to help the bridal party get ready, a particularly close neighbor or a favorite teacher from the bride's or bridegroom's schooldays.

The prime requirement is that it be a quiet, relaxed party that ends at an early hour so everyone involved can get to bed early and get some rest for the big day ahead.

Wedding Day Brunch

If the wedding is scheduled for late afternoon or evening, where and how to serve lunch becomes a real problem. Solve it by serving a buffet luncheon for the bride, her family and attendants.

Since the bridegroom is barred by tradition from seeing his bride on the wedding day before the ceremony, he should not be included. His mother will no doubt want to see to his "last meal" anyway, so the good girl Samaritan can limit her efforts to the distaff side of the wedding.

In the interest of convenience, the bride's home will probably be the best place to serve the food. Check well in advance with her mother on this, then take over all the arrangements yourself. Plan a menu that can be prepared at home and carried to the bride's house. A picnic style meal with one hot dish is an excellent idea for this occasion. It can easily be set up buffet style in the dining room or kitchen.

Provide all the dishes, glasses, mugs, silver, napkins and serving utensils, even sugar, cream, salt and pepper, yourself. Bring your own coffee maker and be sure to keep it going all the time. Serve foods that can be kept for several hours so people can eat whenever there's time.

And, as a final good-will gesture, cart away the dirty dishes to do at home, leaving the house as though the party had never happened.

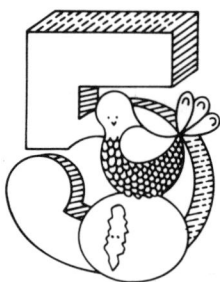

Baby Showers

Whether she's a first or many-time mother, any woman is thrilled when a fuss is made over her expected infant, so baby showers are always in order.

But this time keep the list pared to women only. Men just plain can't *oooh* and *aaah* over tiny garments and if they're around it only spoils the fun for the gals.

Plan a baby shower early enough in pregnancy so the mother-to-be won't be too tired or awkward and so the gifts won't duplicate what she's already accumulated.

Have the party at the time of day mother feels best. Be sure she has a comfortable chair that isn't too low, will support her back and is easy to get in and out of. Please, *please* dispense with any of the hi-jinks that sometimes occur at these parties. Gifts, talk and refreshments are all that's needed.

If the stork arrives before the party, have the shower anyway. Ask the guests to bring unwrapped gifts and appropriate wrapping paper. After everyone has admired all the presents, have each guest wrap hers. The hostess should drop them by the hospital as soon as possible.

A baby shower can even be planned for after the baby's arrival. If you go this route, find out what the mother still needs or wants. One important piece of baby equipment, such as a crib or play pen, is suggested for this kind of party. Each guest can also contribute a prettily wrapped package that contains an inexpensive token gift so there will be more gifts to open.

Whether the party is for a first baby, adopted baby, mother-to-be or new grandma, use all your entertaining wiles to be sure your baby shower is something more than just another pink and blue excuse to get together. It's up to you to see that baby's first social fling is a glorious one, so be ingenious accordingly.

Miscellaneous Baby Shower

If the mother-to-be hasn't started her shopping yet, anything goes in choosing baby gear for a Miscellaneous Shower. But if she's already been raiding the infants' sections, find out what's missing and fill in the gaps.

This can be an informal coffee party at the time of day it's most convenient for all. If it's for a first baby you might want to decorate with mortarboard cap and diploma motif to celebrate the honor guest's graduation to parenthood.

A group gift of a sterilizer and bottles, car bed, play pen, buggy or stroller is always a good idea. Guests may prefer to choose from the multitude of available baby items, including:

divided feeding dish
infant feeding spoon
car bottle warmer (plugs into the cigarette lighter)
spouted drinking cup
subscription to child care magazine
piggy bank with a few coins
adult-size pastel pillowcases (make fine fitted sheets for bassinet)
rattles or small stuffed toys

clothes of all kinds—it's a good idea to choose larger sizes for use
   later
if she knits and you don't, give her the yarn and instructions for a
   baby garment
regular and disposable diapers
padded infant seat-carrier
drying rack
infant nail scissors
mild laundry soap and fabric softener
tongs for handling hot bottles

Stuff small packages into a paper cylinder "diploma" tied with pink and blue ribbons or an outsize graduation cap with a pink and blue tassel. Group larger packages around the container.

Time-of-Day Baby Shower

Assure a variety of gifts and still stick to a definite theme with a Time-of-Day Shower of gifts to use at specific spots on baby's schedule.

Make party time fun with an evening punch or coffee party with easy-to-eat finger foods. Skip a group gift in favor of smaller items presented in a container appropriate to the particular time theme.

Choose from these times and gifts:

MEALTIME—GATHER GIFTS IN AN EMPTY BABY FOOD CASE

cans and jars of baby food and juice
packages of baby cereal
bibs
hand towel for "wipe ups"
feeding spoon
food dishes
cup
bottles and nipples
food-warming pan
disposable nursing kit
suction toy to stand on high-chair tray

NAPTIME—WRAP GIFTS IN A CRIB QUILT

room-darkening window shade
nursery-rhyme coverlet
blanket clips
crib bumper

BATHTIME—BUNDLE GIFTS INTO A DOLL BATHINETTE

towels
washcloths
receiving blankets
soap, oil, cream, lotion and powder
shampoo
plastic bathtub
floating bath thermometer
bath toys
terry or plastic wraparound to protect mother from splashes
cotton swabs
petroleum jelly

PLAYTIME—PILE THE GIFTS INTO A TOY BOX

stuffed animals
rattles
plastic beads
non-tear cloth books
teething ring
play pen pad
walker
crib gym or mobile

VISITING TIME—USE A DIAPER BAG TO HOLD THE GIFTS

rollup nap pad to keep baby from falling off beds
disposable diapers
fancy diaper pins
rubberized flannel lap pads
individual packets of baby cereal
disposable baby bottles
padded infant carrier

brush and comb
car bed
thermo bottle carrier
car bottle warmer
travel kit of oil, powder, soap, lotion, cream and swabs
bunting and cap
sweater
baby blanket

BEDTIME—PLACE PACKAGES ON A TABLE AND COVER WITH A BABY BLANKET

night light
blanket sleeper
extra-heavy night diaper
crib sheets
tiny pillow with cases
crib blanket
cuddly toys
waterproof mattress protector

Nursery Shower

The most important room in the house after baby's arrival will be the nursery, so help get it ready for the newcomer with a Nursery Shower.

Set an ultra-feminine white-clothed tea table for the party, with pink and blue napkins and a centerpiece of rattles and tiny toys which the mother can take home for the newcomer.

If you decide on an expensive item as a group gift, ask each guest to contribute a small toy or rattle so there will be more packages to open. If they decide to give a group gift, consider these:

bassinet
crib
chest of drawers
rocking chair
electric wall clock
folding screen

Bathinette
infant dressing table
vaporizer

Welcome accessories to be given by individuals are:

baby soap, lotion, oil, cream and shampoo
night light
crib mobile
music box
ruffled bassinet cover
Mother Goose wall prints
crib toys
crib bumper
nursery print window curtains
wooden clothes pole
child-size clothes hangers
suitcase style cardboard storage container
toy box
tiny hot water bottle
diaper pail and deodorizer
hamper
light switch plate with nursery decals
wall thermometer
covered containers for cotton balls and swabs
"How Tall Am I?" chart
hanging diaper stacker

Small packages can go into a wicker basket to be used later to hold small accessories, or into a diaper pail.

Sitting Pretty Baby Shower

Long before he can sit up on his own, baby can enjoy observing the world from an upright position if you help him along with a Sitting Pretty Shower of seats and chairs of various kinds.

This is the one baby shower to which you can ask the men, too, as there won't be prolonged opening of baby things. Don't plan anything strenuous (remember the mother-to-be's condition) and think in terms of a weekend brunch, buffet dinner or dessert and coffee.

Collect in advance from the guests, check with the prospective parents to see what equipment they already have, then buy as many of the following as you can:

high chair
stroller
jump chair
car seat
safety chair (hooks onto a table)
seat carrier
potty chair
infant toilet seat
non-tip safety swing
walker
booster seat for dining room chair
rock-or-sit play seat
miniature table and chairs

Wrap the collapsible items with special baby gift wrap and decorate the larger items with festoons of rattles and safety pins.

Shower for the Second Baby

Just because the expected baby isn't the couple's first child is no reason not to celebrate the forthcoming blessed event with a shower. In fact, second (or third or fourth) babies often don't get as many presents as the first arrival, so the mother will be especially appreciative of the fuss made over later arrivals.

Use an ABC decorating theme with a centerpiece of alphabet blocks and ABC books that can go home to the older child, and sprinkle brightly colored cut-out block letters on a white paper tablecloth and napkins.

Joint gifts are popular at this kind of shower: a gift certificate for baby's first portrait, a savings account or government bond, subscription to a diaper service or a gift certificate at her favorite store so mother can refurbish her leftover layette with things she needs now.

Otherwise, concentrate on items that have appeared on the market since the older child's arrival or on things that can't be passed down too successfully, such as:

extra feeding bottles
nipples
bottle caps
diapers
booties
crib shoes and socks
teething toys
gold baby ring
rectal thermometer
bottle and nipple brushes
rumble seat for stroller
baby aspirin
fancy diaper pins
cuddly toys
rattles
plastic pants

Put the gifts in a large box decorated like a giant building block or with colorful alphabet letters glued all over it.

Shower for an Adopted Baby

By all means shower gifts on an adopted baby. For once, you'll know for sure whether the gifts are for a boy or girl!

No matter what the time of year, a Mother's Day theme is particularly appropriate with pink or blue décor. However, skip the stork decorations. Use tiny dolls or toy soldiers in the table decorations and pop them into a paper bag for mother to take home as an extra gift.

Any of the group or individual gift ideas given for the other baby showers in this book are appropriate for this party, but it's a good idea to check first to see what the new mother needs.

As a special memento of the party, buy a baby book and have each of the guests sign it during the party. Mother can fill in the vital statistics herself.

Shower for Absent Honorée

With so many families on the move these days, many expectant mothers are no longer living near their old friends when they're expecting their babies. If this is the case with a good friend of yours, give her a shower anyway.

Have the guests bring their unwrapped gifts and gift paper to the party. After the gifts have been admired by all, have each guest wrap her package. Then you mail them to the absent honorée.

It's a good idea to wait until baby's arrival so larger sizes for boy or girl may be selected in case the baby is already supplied with infant clothing. Specify only small, lightweight gifts to lessen shipping headaches.

The faraway mother will welcome your interest in her baby and will enjoy receiving:

sweaters
socks
footed sleepers
rattles or tiny stuffed animals
plastic pants
stretch terrycloth jump suits
mittens
knit caps
undershirts
receiving blankets
washcloths
corduroy crawlers
tee shirts
diaper liners
teething toys
nursery decals
gold baby ring
diaper pins
bootee sox
bibs
crib sheets

As your gift, provide a baby book which each of the guests can sign. Immediately after the party ship the gift carton to the guest of honor and write to her, telling her about the party in detail, so she can share in the fun. If one of the group can bring a camera, pictures taken at the party will also be treasured by the absent honorée.

Showers for Mother Herself

By the time a woman has had a baby or two she usually has most of the baby things she needs. Or perhaps the expectant mother you want to fete has already been inundated with baby things at other parties. There's no reason to bypass a shower in cases like these. Give gifts for the mother-to-be herself. Here are four ideas which should make a hit with a special expectant mother at a morning coffee, luncheon, tea or evening dessert.

HOSPITAL BAG

Send mother to the hospital in style by having your guests pile the things she will need into a roomy tote bag. Make a list of essentials and have guests sign up for gifts. Some will probably want to shop together for matched fragrances.

Choose a handsome bag which will be your gift and suggest the following to fill it:

bed jacket—a batik print or citrus stripes (perhaps stitched up by its donor) is more fun than the conventional frills
ruffled nightcap
hand mirror
spray or stick cologne
aerosol body powder
scented body lotion
hair spray
eye shadow pallette
plastic case with toothbrush, paste and mouthwash
false eyelashes—what better time to learn to fiddle with them?
case of several demi-size lipsticks, coordinating nail polish
facial soap in plastic container
stationery, pen and stamps
clutch of current magazines
popular paperback novels
eyeshade for napping
rent a television set for her hospital stay
arrange for a professional manicurist the day after the baby arrives

Pack the gifts in the tote or pile them on a card table.

FINALLY, THE TENTH MONTH!

Make coping with her presently awkward abdomen easier for the mother-to-be by giving her a shower of post-baby size belts, blouses and accessories. The prospect of wearing new clothes soon will make the last weeks of waiting a little less tedious, and she can even use some of the jewelry and scarves to perk up her by now monotonous maternity wardrobe.

Be sure your clothing gifts recognize the reemergence of her waistline. High style and low maintenance are important, so choose from easy-care fabrics and freewheeling designs.

cotton pullovers in bright and basic colors
belted sweater vest
turtleneck dickies
tailored shirts or shells
loopy leather belts
ropes of pearls, metals and beads for waist or neck
clanky bracelets
pins that shout their presence
oblong, triangular and smoke ring scarves
a handful of rings
earrings—from the simplest to the most dangling

Pack the gifts in a straw or fabric carryall she can use later for shopping.

MOTHER'S HELPER

One of the most useful parties you can plan is a shower of pledges for a given number of hours of help at home to make the first weeks less hectic.

The new mother will be delighted to count on her friends for:

1 or 2 hours of housework
a basket of ironing
a dinner invitation for the family while she's in the hospital
a trip to the grocery store for weekly shopping
a promise to take the older children to a movie, the park or other
   outing during baby's first days home
doing a round of mother's weekly errands

a specified number of hours of help of mother's choosing emptying
the mending basket
chauffeuring for baby's early checkups at the doctor's office
helping the family polish the house for her arrival home from the
hospital
standby assistance during baby's first bath

List the promises on a sheet of paper with the donor's name and
phone number for easy reference.

On the Town Shower

Include the prospective father in the festivities by giving the
couple their first night out after the baby arrives.
Since this is a gift for the two of them, make the party for both and
invite the men for a dessert tasting.
Go all out on gifts so they'll have a chance to celebrate the baby's
arrival lavishly without completely destroying their strained budget.
Gifts chosen from this list will ensure a night to remember:

certificate for dinner at their favorite restaurant
florist's order for a corsage and boutonnière
tokens or certificate for parking lot, or cash for taxi fare
movie, concert or theatre tickets
three lanes of bowling each
a pair of admissions to a special museum exhibit, art show or other
event they might not get to see otherwise
a promise to hire a baby sitter or to sit yourself
chits for a nightcap, midnight coffee or snack
dime for a call to check with the baby sitter
bottle of champagne or wine for a special celebration toast
a pair of champagne goblets or wineglasses to drink the toast

Since most of the gifts will be certificates or admission tickets,
enclose them in clever studio cards and present them in a "mail
pouch" fashioned from a pillowcase.

Shower for the Father-to-Be

If there's an expectant father where you work, give him a shower
at lunchtime or right after work.

Have everyone bring his lunch or order food sent in. Decorate his office or desk with festoons of huge safety pins, rattles or swathes of diapers.

A department store or specialty shop gift certificate is the safest choice for the group to give. Then have each person add a gag gift. Or you can give him a gift certificate for baby's portrait and a desk frame to hold it.

For fun, be sure he receives:

large bottle of aspirin
ear plugs
paperback baby care book
an alarm clock for the 2 A.M. feeding
diapers
safety pins
baby powder
rubberized flannel lap pad
"bragging book" of snapshot size photo holders
feeding spoon
warm slippers for walking the baby at night
box of baby laundry powder

Fold a piece of white cloth into a diaper shape to hold the gifts or nest the packages in a box decorated with expectant and new father cartoons.

Shower for the New Grandmother

The first-time prospective grandmother has probably been so busy carting gifts to baby's home, she hasn't given a thought to what will happen when baby comes to visit her. She's surely disposed of all her own baby things long ago, so she needs a shower of gifts that will come in handy when baby comes to her house.

This can be a mother-daughter party with cards or conversation. Have the gift opening just before refreshments. Or the grandmother's own friends may prefer to give the shower for just their own group. Either way, take a cavalier attitude toward calories, even though Grandmother *isn't* eating for two, and serve the poshest dessert you can concoct.

Ask for individual gifts for this shower, things that are fun to buy and still practical to have on hand, such as:

infant feeding spoon
non-tip feeding dish
baby cup
bibs
cans and jars of baby food
feeding bottles and nipples
rattles and small stuffed animals
toy box
sweater and cap
a dozen diapers
plastic pants
terry stretch jump suit
safety strap or bed-top napper to make any bed safe for baby
baby oil, lotion, powder and cream
cotton balls and swabs

If your husband or beau can build an old-fashioned cradle, make this your gift and arrange the other presents in it. Or paint a cardboard box in baby pastels and decorate it with nursery decals.

Other Kinds of Showers

There are other important milestones in life that can be marked with a party and a shower of gifts.

While these occasions are not showers in the traditional sense, they fulfill the same purpose as wedding and baby showers: to send the honor guest into a new phase of his life with the love and best wishes of those close to him.

The same standards that apply to other showers govern these parties: limit the invitations to close friends or, in some cases, only to relatives; choose the type of party your guests will most enjoy; plan carefully, and work ahead. Then join your guests and enjoy the party.

Off to College Shower

Going away to school conjures up thoughts of trunks full of clothes and accessories. But there's another important aspect of college shopping—dorm room accessories and study aids—which are fun to give to the student and a budget saver for parents.

Remember that other young people and their parents have heavy expenses of their own at this time and a gift might be a burden. So it's best to keep this a relatives-only party. Then it can double as a good-bye get-together for the honor guest and his family.

Plan a late summer picnic or an evening dessert and coffee party. If the party is indoors, use a back-to-school theme in decorating: books, horn rim glasses, school pennants, railroad or airline timetables and toy suitcases.

If several people want to band together to get a popcorn popper, blender or small coffee maker, check first to be sure appliances are allowed in the dorm rooms. Other good group gifts are an electric toothbrush, portable record player or tape recorder. A young man should welcome an electric shaver, while a girl can use electric curlers, a hair drier or a facial sauna. Or you might ask everyone to chip in for a gift certificate for a store in the college town so the student can choose a bedspread, curtains or other fillips to dress up college-furnished quarters.

Gifts from this list should help the departing student feel more at home in his new quarters and many of them will bolster his dwindling allowance when he's out on his own:

high intensity study lamp
alarm clock
laundry bag
writing paper
stamped envelopes and postal cards
paperback reference books—dictionary, thesaurus, atlas and encyclopedia
pens, pencils and erasers
book bag
notebook, typing and carbon paper
scratch pads
reinforcements
file folders
paper clips
thumbtacks
ruler

cellophane and masking tape
bulletin board
bookends
rubber cement, paste and glue
clip board
typewriter dust cover
piggy bank
wig stand
throw pillows
pencil holder
camera film
plastic snack set
can and bottle opener
first aid kit
sewing kit
iron-on patches in assorted colors
soap and soap dish
toothpaste, mouthwash and dental floss
shampoo and hair-setting gel
hair spray
safety pins
slippers or dorm boots
curler caddy
laundry marking pencil
iron-on name tags
posters
records
typewriter ribbons
tape recorder cartridges or reels
snack or can opener cookbook
teabags
dehydrated soups
envelopes of dip seasoning
cube sugar
powdered cream
freeze-dried coffee
canned meat spreads
plug-in water heating unit

Pack smaller gifts in a soft-side suitcase or wrap them hobo fashion in a bandana tied to a broom handle. Paint a covered tin bread box in school colors to hold food gifts.

First Apartment Shower

The newly employed young man or woman who is setting up housekeeping for the first time will welcome a shower of gifts to make that first studio or furnished apartment more livable.

Choose gifts from the Kitchen Basics, Closet, Bathroom or Off to College showers. Or chip in for a gift certificate from a leading department store so the honoré can fill his or her own needs.

Entering the Service Shower

While this party is usually given for the young man or woman going into one of the Armed Forces, it is equally applicable for anyone going into the Peace Corps or other foreign assignment or one of the volunteer service organizations based in this country.

Have a buffet dinner, cookout, picnic or beach party, depending on your facilities and the time of year. You might want to put up a huge "Good-bye, Good Luck" banner, but otherwise don't decorate. Instead, allow lots of time for the party so the honor guest can have a chance to say his good-byes to all. Make good food and plenty of it the core of the gathering.

The departing guest will be traveling light, so don't load him down with a lot of gear he'll have no place to store and which he can probably buy cheaper in government stores. The most useful gift you can choose is money, so take up a collection and give him the cash tucked into a farewell card which all the guests have signed.

As hostess you might add a pocket address book with the names and addresses of the guests entered in the alphabetical sections. And extract a promise from each guest to write the honor guest a letter during the first month he's away.

Welcome Home Shower

The far better side of the going away coin is a celebration to welcome the honor guest back home at the end of his tour of duty.

Again make it an informal gathering with all his favorite people and food awaiting him. And again limit the decorations to a blatant banner proclaiming his return.

If you really know what he wants and needs for his new life after service, then greet him with gift-wrapped packages. But hard cash or a gift certificate at his favorite store is probably the smartest way to handle the gift selection.

Moving Away Shower

Say good-bye to friends who are moving to another city with a farewell get-together of the local gang.

For this party include whole families—the children will want to say good-bye, too—and make it a buffet dinner with all the guests indicating in advance what they'll bring. Make the starting hour as early as possible so you'll have plenty of time for the party and the travelers can still get a good night's rest before beginning their trip.

Carry the moving theme into the decorations by using toy moving vans, trunks and suitcases for the table centerpieces and hang road maps, posters of the area in which the family will live and hand-lettered farewell signs on the walls.

Keep the gifts small and packable, such as these:

FOR THE CAR:

emergency lantern lamp
flashlight with extra batteries
warning flares
emergency tire inflater
dry-chemical fire extinguisher
length of rope
orange hunter's gloves to signal trouble and protect hands
small shovel
spray window cleaner
roll of paper towels
magnetic coin holder for instrument panel with coins for tolls or
    phone calls
first aid kit
whisk broom

84

6-inch long 2x4 wooden blocks for changing tires on hills
screwdriver
windshield scraper or aerosol defroster if the climate is cold
sponge in plastic bag
litter bucket or bags
umbrella
facial tissues
empty gasoline can

FOR THE FAMILY EN ROUTE:

picnic lunch for the first day
road map with most direct route clearly marked
information on tourist attractions along the way
paper cups and napkins
large size water or cold drink jug
can and bottle opener
scratch pads and pencils
coloring books and crayons if there are small children
games with magnetic counters to play in the car
spiral notebook for each child with his name written on the cover
children's books
paperback novels for adults to read at night
cans of cookies and snacks
drawstring laundry bag

TO USE WHEN THEY GET THERE:

change-of-address cards
address book with names and addresses of friends they are leaving
    behind
subscriptions to old and new hometown papers
tourist material on their new town—can be ordered in advance
    from the Chamber of Commerce
any contacts you may have in their new area
photo album with pictures of their old friends
personalized gifts to be autographed by all at the party—a baseball
    or football for boys, autograph album or signature stuffed ani-
    mal for girls, books for the adults (cookbook, garden guide for

85

plants in the new area, home repair guide, history or travel book on the new area)

send letters of introduction to friends in the new town and give carbon copies of the letters to honor guests at the party

Since the departing family will probably be going by car, pack auto safety and other travel accessories in a small but sturdy box they can stow in the car. A wicker picnic case or zippered carryall will hold travel accessory gifts now and be a visible reminder of your friendship later. Gifts for their new home can be packed in a shipping carton which the hostess can mail to their new address.

New Neighbors Shower

Welcome newcomers to your neighborhood by inviting them to dinner on moving day.

Ask each "old timer" family to contribute to a buffet dinner and include the children so whole families can get acquainted.

Choose as gifts things they are likely to need right away, none of them expensive, which will come in handy during the settling-in process and often prevent frantic trips to the hardware store:

electric light bulbs
picture wire
assorted size nails
hammer
screwdriver
paper plates, cups and napkins
ashtrays
huge plastic garbage bags
latest editions of the local papers
frozen casseroles with heating instructions
a list of useful names, addresses and phone numbers: doctor, hospital, plumber, veterinarian, the nearest grocery and hardware stores, recommended department and specialty stores, hairdresser, barber, restaurants, taxi and shoe repairman and cleaner
offer to baby sit while mother is unpacking

map of the area with schools, shopping centers, hospital and other important places marked

state map and area tourist attraction booklets

Pack the presents into paper cartons for easy carrying home.

As a variation, instead of inviting the family to dinner, take their first meal to them. Have the same planned potluck from the neighbors and include the carton of gifts, each with the donor's name, address and phone number clearly marked. Saying "thank you" will give the newcomers a chance to get acquainted after their initial settling in.

Home Decorating Shower

If someone you know is renovating an older home or moving into another apartment, they'll appreciate the help of a shower of decorating tools.

If they need assistance in the actual painting and decorating, ask the guests to show up in old clothes, ready to lend a hand. After—but only after—the work is done, bring out the refreshments and have a party.

If they need financial assistance rather than willing workers, have a buffet dinner and ask everyone to chip in for a gift certificate at the town's leading department store so they can spend the cash on what they need to pull their project together.

If they have to start getting equipment from scratch, give them:

paint brush—including the new throwaway ones with refills
disposable paint buckets
paint rollers and trays
certificates for paint and varnish
fast-drying primer
paint thinner
varnish remover
putty knife
masking tape
spatter cloths
stepladder stool
painter's caps

sandpaper
cheesecloth
paint rags
antiquing kits

Wrap the gifts in a spatter cloth or line up the packages on the steps of a ladder. A gift certificate can be concealed in an empty paint can or bucket or tucked into the band of a painter's cap.

Tenth Anniversary Shower

It takes just about ten years for the limited-life wedding gifts to disappear completely and this usually comes along when rising family costs render the budget ill-equipped to handle replacements. Celebrate the honored couple's tenth wedding anniversary by re-equipping them with replacements.

Make this a couple's party, and key decorations to the anniversary theme. The tenth anniversary is tin, so check the pre-wedding can shower plan for decorating suggestions.

Don't give a group gift. Replenish dwindling supplies of:

towels
washcloths
sheets
pillowcases
glasses
ashtrays
throw rugs
pot holders
the latest in kitchen gadgets

A huge plastic wastebasket or laundry sorter will hold the gifts now, come in handy later.

Individual Parties

Once you've decided the kind of shower you'll give, plans for the party itself become paramount. While the type of shower will determine to some extent the mode and mood of the party, you'll still have lots of flexibility in how, what and when to serve.

Leisurely, talky and bountiful, breakfast is a popular way to entertain mixed groups on weekend mornings. Its first cousin—brunch—is even better for sleepyheads who don't like to get started very early in the day. Keep the atmosphere gay and informal and while you can use flowers or fruit for a centerpiece, don't put candles on the table. Save them for after five when they're needed to provide light. You can accommodate a fairly large number without too much fuss if you serve buffet and don't try too complicated a menu. For any party, incidentally, it's more important to provide plenty of what you do have rather than try for too varied a repast.

Skip luncheons for the men and save them for the gals. Keep the meal light—you may serve three courses but two will do nicely—and have the first course on the table before you seat your guests. You can handle a larger group with a buffet or tray luncheon but a sit down meal is nicest for really special occasions. Again, use flowers or fruit for a centerpiece, but no candles.

Tea, that most feminine of daytime social activities, gets many votes as a favorite afternoon party, but coffee parties at all hours of the day are gaining in popularity. An evening coffee tasting might prove a new experience for your group and will test your ingenuity as a hostess.

Dinner possibilities are virtually limitless, so choose the kind and style you can handle best. Memorable meals range from the most informal outdoor picnic to the carefully served dress-up dinner, with candles on the table and lots of beautiful silver and china.

If you can't manage a complete dinner, try some of the other evening parties suggested here. You'll be surprised how many people you can serve successfully.

If you're serving foreign food, make the setting as compatible with the foreign theme as you can. Get information and posters from foreign information services, the United Nations, travel agencies and your local library. Import and specialty shops can provide serving equipment and accessories. Get recipes and ideas from foreign restaurants, ethnic cookbooks and home service magazines.

Whatever food you serve, have plenty of it and serve it attractively. Be sure hot foods are really hot, cold foods thoroughly chilled. Don't experiment with new recipes—always have a trial run when preparing any dish before you serve it to guests. Keep your facilities and your budget in mind when planning your party, and don't overextend either.

You will note that many of the party plans in this book suggest cocktails, mixed drinks, wine or beer. If your own preferences or community customs do not include serving alcoholic beverages, merely eliminate them from your plans. In any event, always provide a non-alcoholic alternative for non-drinking guests; and, whatever you do, don't apologize or explain.

When you do serve drinks have a reliable recipe, use good ingredients, measure accurately and follow directions carefully. Except for offbeat or special drinks, no cocktail recipes are given here. These vary from community to community, so serve what's customary in your own area.

If your party date is on or near a special holiday, it's fun to tie in special events. Valentine's Day, Washington's Birthday, St. Patrick's Day, Easter and Thanksgiving are so familiar that they haven't been covered here. So look to the more offbeat holidays as a way of adding verve to your party.

In addition to the holiday themes suggested in this book, investigate dates of local or regional importance (the Battle of New Orleans, the Great Chicago Fire, the Boston Tea Party or the anniversary of your state's admission to the union, for example). Look up some of these lesser known holidays and events in the library. Then combine guidelines set up in this book with your own ideas to come up with the most original parties in your crowd.

Recipes for dishes marked * in the party plans are given in the recipe section of this book.

Buffet Breakfast

Do your own version of the traditional English breakfast. If you have room set the food on a sideboard or auxiliary table and seat your guests around the dining table.

If your table won't accommodate all the guests at one sitting, ask them to find places in the living room. Some will be content to sit on the floor, while others can occupy the sofa, chairs, even borrowed stools. If you don't have table or standing tray space for everyone, don't serve meat that must be cut with a knife. Try bite-size sausages.

Encourage everyone to return for seconds and expect them to linger over final cups of coffee.

Serve foods that can be kept warm in a chafing dish or on an electric warming tray. You can even bring the breakfast meats to the buffet in the electric skillet. Keep hot breads warm in napkin-wrapped servers.

Be sure there's plenty of coffee and make a pot of tea for those who may prefer it.

MENU

Fruit Juice
Bacon, Ham or Sausage   Scrambled Eggs
Hot Buttered Biscuits   Jam   Heated Danish Pastries
Coffee, Tea

Pancake Breakfast

Serve that old breakfast standby, pancakes, but let individuality shine through by providing a choice of toppings.

The mere addition of juice, breakfast meat and coffee will make a marvelously satisfying meal. You'll find the toppings suggested here in your supermarket or gourmet shop, but have at least one pitcher of homemade syrup to show off your culinary prowess.

Serve buffet with the syrups in pretty pitchers, the toppings on a lazy susan for easy access.

MENU

Fruit Juice   Sausage, Ham or Bacon
Pancakes*   Butter Pats   Homemade Maple Syrup*
Blueberry Syrup Honey   Apricot Marmalade
Sweetened Crushed Strawberries
Coffee, Tea

Champagne Breakfast

The absolute can't-do-withouts for this party are elegance and plenty of time. Set as elaborate a table as you can: white cloth, large matching napkins, all the ornate servers you possess, silver and crystal everywhere.

While the menu itself is simple, the service must be impeccable, so it's best if the party is for no more than eight. Start with a glass of champagne, refill the glasses during the various courses, have a final glass of wine, then coffee.

Use long-stemmed champagne glasses (no plastic ones for this party) and ask your guests to dress up. This is the time for you to wear a glamorous hostess gown or at-home pants, with a frilly apron for the last-minute cooking.

Delegate a man to open the champagne so you won't have to struggle with an obstreperous cork, and be sure the wine is iced properly: lay the bottle on its side for three hours in the refrigerator or chill on cracked ice (in a silver wine cooler, if possible) for 30 minutes before serving. There are approximately seven glasses in a fifth of champagne.

Provide gingerale for any non-drinking guests. It looks the same and bubbles just as prettily when poured.

MENU

Fresh or Frozen Strawberries   Broiled Bacon
Scrambled Eggs with Mushrooms*   Buttered Biscuits
Jelly or Jam
Champagne   Coffee

Sunday Brunch

A lazed-out party that combines the best of breakfast and lunch, a Sunday Brunch can be a most elegant way of entertaining.

Greet your guests with a drink and have hot coffee on hand for the poor souls who barely have their eyes open. Serve buffet if you like, but be sure everyone has a comfortable spot in which to roost while eating.

Feed your guests a special egg dish and be sure there are pots and pots of coffee for those who want to linger just to talk or to watch a special sports event on television.

MENU

Screwdrivers, Bloody Marys or Milk Punch*   Fruit Juice
Empress Eggs*   Buttered Toast
Canadian Style Bacon
Coffee

Coffee Parties

A distinctly American contribution to the entertainment scene, the coffee party can easily be adjusted to your requirements. For ladies only or men included, from early morning until just before midnight, coffee, accompanied by an array of tempting foods or a single type of sweet roll, means conviviality. Serve it with utmost formality or carefree "come as you are." Build your shower around a coffee party and brew enjoyment of the occasion as well as of the beverage.

SIMPLE MORNING COFFEE

A wonderful choice for old friends or neighbors who enjoy a relaxed chat, this is an easy party for hostess and guests alike. Keep things simple, but fuss enough so the guests will feel they're at a party.

Start early enough so you'll have plenty of time for the festivities without running into lunchtime. Get going the night before: set the table with cups and saucers, a tray for the coffeepot, cream pitcher, filled sugar bowl, spoons and napkins and a pitcher and small tumblers for juice. Cover the partially set table with a large sheet you can whip off in the morning.

Then the morning of the party all you'll need to do is pour the juice, make coffee, heat and butter the breakfast breads and greet your guests.

A choice of heated breakfast breads will eliminate the need for extra plates and knives and simplify serving. Be sure to have lots of hot coffee to serve as long as your guests want it.

MENU

Chilled Fruit Juice
Coffee Cake   Buttered Muffins
Doughnut Holes*
Coffee

SUNDAY MORNING COFFEE

Expand your weekday morning coffee to include the men by having the party on Sunday morning. You'll probably want to have more of a variety, but stick to food that doesn't require extra plates and silverware.

By all means serve fruit juice, but since this isn't a substantial meal resist the impulse to add vodka to the juice. Stick to basic "coffee and."

MENU

Chilled Orange and Tomato Juice
Assorted Danish Pastries   Doughnuts
Coffee Cake   Buttered Biscuits
Spiced Pineapple Chunks*   Coffee

AFTERNOON COFFEE

Make this party as elegant as high tea. Center the serving table
with flowers and scatter other small floral arrangements wherever
you can. Use your nicest tablecloth, china and silver, and ask friends
to pour.

In addition to coffee and perhaps a pot of chocolate, set out
platters and trays of party sandwiches and cakes, and dishes of nuts
and mints. For serving you'll need dessert plates, forks and napkins,
so be sure to have them ready.

MENU

Assorted Tea Sandwiches*   Apple Cake*
Assorted Cookies   Sugared Pineapple Cubes or Strawberries*
Salted Nuts   Mints
Coffee   Hot Chocolate

COFFEE TASTING

Don't be too quick to assume that a cup of well-brewed, steaming
hot coffee is the only kind to serve at your party. Be adventurous and
branch out with a Coffee Tasting party, a special hit with the men.
You'll find guests receptive to trying different blends, brews and
ways of serving what will no longer be a familiar cup of coffee.

Serve with verve from a large table with regular coffee at one end,
espresso at the other. In the middle, station bowls and dishes of sugar
cubes, plain and whipped cream, lemon and orange twists, chocolate
curls, cinnamon, nutmeg and any other special ingredients your coffees require.

Keep the food simple and not too sweet, as the coffees are likely to
be rich themselves. And provide cups of regular coffee for any timid
souls you may discover in your midst.

95

MENU

Viennese Coffee *   Mocha Java*
Café au Rhum*   Mexican Coffee*
Café Cacao*   Espresso
Café au Lait*   Caffé Cappuccino*
Café à l'Orange*   Roman Espresso*
Irish Coffee*   Caffé Borgia*
Café Royal*   Caffé Cioccolata*
Café à la Mode*   Iced Coffee*

Demitasse

Thinly Sliced, Buttered Nut, Orange and Raisin Breads
After Dinner Mints   Salted Nuts

Tray Luncheon

A Tray Luncheon is a marvelous way to handle a large group as it enables you to serve quickly and easily with a minimum of fuss and commotion.

The trick in planning a tray luncheon is to choose foods that can be eaten easily, as everything except dessert goes onto the tray before serving and guests must be able to hold the trays in their laps without having to maneuver.

Make your own lap trays by spray-painting variety store cookie sheets. Line each with a paper doily, add a napkin and your table is set.

To distribute the food, line up the filled trays on the dining table or kitchen counter, whichever works out best, and let each guest pick up her own. When it's time to serve dessert, ask each person to stack her tray on a side table provided for this purpose and then pick up her dessert plate from the original serving point.

You, and perhaps a helper or two, can circulate with coffee and extra rolls.

MENU

Chilled Tomato Juice   Cheese Sticks*
Molded Seafood Salad*   Tiny Buttered Rolls
          Olives and Carrot Sticks
      Angel Food Cake   Coffee

Buffet Salad Luncheon

Equally good for an indoor or outdoor party, a Buffet Salad Luncheon gives the guests a chance to choose their own favorites.

Those who don't know each other very well can start conversations by comparing notes on how they've combined ingredients in the "mix-your-own" and speculate on what is in some of the ready-mixed salads.

Since it's difficult to chase bits of lettuce or elusive elbows of macaroni around a plate balanced on the lap, provide seating at card tables or with individual stand-trays for each guest.

Load the flower-centered buffet table with as many different salads as you can. The guests then take some of each, perhaps returning for more of those they particularly like.

To avoid excessive foot traffic, set cups at the individual places, then pour coffee or tea for each guest after she's seated. Dessert can be served from an auxiliary table or passed on trays.

Because everyone will be sampling several salads, estimate smaller than usual servings when preparing the salads.

MENU

Mix-Your-Own Salad*   Sour Cream Potato Salad*
Cottage Cheese and Fruits   Fruit Salad Dressing*
Chicken Salad   Curried Rice Salad*
Stuffed Eggs   Olives   Celery and Carrot Sticks
Individual Wedding Cakes*
Coffee   Tea

Indoor or Outdoor Lawn Party

An informal Lawn Luncheon doesn't require a pretty garden. It doesn't even have to have a lawn. What it does need is an outdoor atmosphere, one that you can create inside if you must.

If you have a big yard, chances are you have the equipment you need for entertaining in it. But if you're housebound because of the weather, the time of year or because you live in an apartment, don't let it stop you. Bring the garden atmosphere inside and let blossoms brighten your party. The food for a garden party can be the same, regardless of its location, and it's surprising just how outdoorsy you can make your living room.

Push back or clear out as much of your regular furniture as you can and use lounge chairs, small tables and lots of plants to simulate a garden. Hang or scatter big paper flowers, set the table with a flower-sprinkled cloth and napkins and use posy-hued paper plates.

Carry the informality into the serving: colorful serving dishes on brick trivets, straw baskets for breadsticks, wooden-handled salad servers and colorful wooden or ceramic salt and pepper shakers.

MENU

Deviled Crab in Patty Shells*   Breadsticks
Tossed Green Salad with French Dressing
Sherbet or Fruit Cup   Sesame Cookies*
Coffee   Iced Tea

Sit-Down Luncheon

This party should be feminine, formal and luxurious. And, since everyone is seated at a single table, it is also small and intimate.

This is the time to bring out your nicest things: a full tablecloth with matching napkins, freshly polished silver, flowers for the center-piece and your nicest china and serving dishes.

Since this is a special party, you'll probably want to serve three courses instead of the more usual two. Make serving simpler by offering the first course in the living room. Then when the guests come to the table, the main course can be in place and you'll have to clear only for dessert.

After lunch it's a nice idea to invite everyone to have another cup of coffee in the living room where they can chat comfortably and you won't have to worry about the final table clearing until after the party.

MENU

Cream of Tomato Soup in Mugs   Cheese Puffs*
Crab Louis*   Hot Buttered Rolls
Lemon Pie   Coffee

Tea Parties

From a simple table in a corner of the living room to an elaborately set dining table complete with endless varieties of food, afternoon tea is still a favorite way to entertain.

Use flowers, your nicest cloth, delicate china cups and your most impressive serving pieces. Always serve the traditional something hot, something cold and something sweet, and be sure to have plenty. Some hostesses feel three or four goodies per person is enough, but five or even six is safer.

To perk up the best brand of tea you can buy, try some of these variations: stir with a stick of cinnamon, serve with slices of lime and orange as well as the usual lemon, or place a sprig of fresh mint or a couple of whole cloves in the teapot. In the summer you may want to offer tall glasses of mint-topped iced tea as well as hot tea.

To cut cake into finger-manageable pieces, cut it first into half slices, then into narrower pieces that can be picked up and eaten easily.

SIMPLE TEA

You'll need only one person to pour for a small number of guests, so set the table where she'll be able to serve easily and chat with the guests while they are eating.

On a tray before the pourer place a teapot, cream pitcher, sugar bowl and waste bowl to empty the remains of the first cup before she pours a second. Place cups, saucers and spoons on one side of the tray, napkins and plates of food from which the guests can serve themselves on the other. To avoid traffic jams at the table, you may want to pass food to the guests after they have been served tea and are seated about the room.

MENU

Hot Buttered Muffins or Hot Buttered Biscuits
Nut Bread and Butter Sandwiches   Slivers of Pound Cake

Salted Nuts   Mints
Tea*

HIGH TEA

Serve High Tea in the grand manner. Center the table with flowers and place smaller bouquets throughout the party area.

Center the table so traffic can go on both sides, cover the table with a heavy white cloth and use every bit of lovely china, crystal and silver that you can in serving. Move out all the extra dining room chairs, leaving only one at each end for the pourers. At one end of the table set a large tray (sans cloth) with a teapot, cream pitcher, sugar bowl and waste bowl (all silver, if possible) and arrange cups, saucers and spoons on either side of the tray with piles of tea napkins near the cups.

At the opposite end, serve hot chocolate. Next to the chocolate pot place a bowl of whipped cream and another of shaved milk chocolate so the pourer can top each cup of chocolate with a dollop of whipped cream and a sprinkle of chocolate shavings. Arrange cups, saucers, spoons and napkins, though not so many, at each side.

Have stacks of small plates near the trays and platters of food, and don't serve anything that must be eaten with a fork. Concentrate on bite-size and miniature foods that can be easily handled with the fingers. Serve at least six varieties of cold and sweet foods and three hot. Have enough helpers to keep dishes replenished and rotate pourers so no one has to sit too long.

MENU

HOT FOODS

Cinnamon Toast Fingers   Tiny Buttered Muffins
Buttered Biscuits   Hot Cheese Puffs*
Sesame-Butter Sticks*   Anchovy Biscuits*

COLD FOODS

Boston Brown Bread Spread with Cream Cheese
Lightly Buttered Banana, Nut, Date or Orange Bread
Assorted Small Sandwiches*

SWEET FOODS

Pound Cake   Fruitcake*
Individual Iced Cakes* Sponge Cake
Petits Fours   Filled Cookies
Gingerbread Squares Miniature Cream Puffs
Scotch Shortbread Cookies
Tea*   Hot Chocolate

Cocktail Party

To cater to a crowd without losing your mind, give the most smashing Cocktail Party ever. Dramatic yet flexible, the cocktail party is a wonderful way for a single hostess to entertain twelve to twenty, while several can combine their talents to produce a smash success for as many as fifty.

To avoid having the party stretch on into infinity, be specific about time length in the invitations (two or three hours is plenty long enough) and slow down on food and drink service as the witching hour approaches. No Cinderella you, but if you don't want the party to swing past the dinner hour you'll have to guide your guests subtly on their way before they get too giddy or too famished. Otherwise you'll find yourself frantically scrambling eggs or making sandwiches and destroying your image as the perfectly prepared, unflappable hostess.

Don't try for too much variety in drinks or food. Ask several men to serve as bartenders. Rotate them so they won't have to work the whole time and miss the party, and make up a definite schedule so everyone knows who's working when.

Unless you have plenty of kitchen help, forget about hot hors d'oeuvres and serve only make-aheads with plenty of replacements in reserve. Have more than enough liquor, glasses, ice and mix and be sure to have something for the non-drinkers. Apple juice is different and refreshing, or you may decide to stick to the more conventional tomato juice or soft drinks.

The whole matter of drinks is so complex and depends so much on the customs and tastes of your guests and community that we'll deal with it only superficially here.

Have a conference with your liquor store man about kinds and quantities, bearing in mind that half-gallons are cheapest, then quarts, then fifths. Caution the bartenders not to make drinks overly strong so your guests won't misjudge their usual capacity.

The day before the party, clean house, set up the bar, fill cigarette boxes, distribute matches, coasters and ashtrays and move small pieces of furniture out of traffic patterns. Keep table tops clear and put away any fragile bric-a-brac.

Your bar can be two card tables pushed together or a desk covered with a full-length cloth. Set it up so the bartender faces the guests, but be sure it doesn't block the main line of traffic.

Place glasses at one end of the bar and a sampling of liquor being offered at the other. The bar should also hold a cocktail shaker or pitcher, pitcher of water, bottle opener, cocktail napkins, a stack of bar or dish towels and bowls of any special garnishes or ingredients needed for the drinks, such as lemon peel, cherries, orange slices, olives, onions, limes, sugar or bitters. Store extra glasses, liquor and mix on a small table or bookshelf behind the bar. Extra bottles can even go under the table.

Serve the food from a table set away from the bar and scatter bowls of olives (without pits if you don't want to pick up strays for the next three days!), nuts and popcorn through the party area.

Do as much advance food preparation as you can: make and refrigerate pâté, dips and spreads, cut raw vegetables, cook shrimp and have nuts, popcorn and crackers ready. Get plain round wooden or plastic trays from the dime store to supplement your own supply and use china plates and platters for refrigerated foods.

In case your guests are hungrier than you expected, have in reserve the makings of an antipasto tray (canned rolled anchovies and artichoke hearts, slices of bologna and salami, some celery sticks and cherry tomatoes), plus cheese spread and a loaf or two of sliced icebox rye. Don't bother with individual canapés or pre-spread crackers—it just complicates your party day.

Early on the morning of the party, arrange the flowers, place refrigerated foods in serving dishes and cover with transparent wrap. Have bowls and trays for nonperishable foods ready to be filled. Then a couple of hours before the party, get out trays and bowls, crackers and other nonperishables, set out cheese spreads to soften, arrange the chips and crackers for dips and make a quick check of cigarettes, ashtrays, matches and napkins.

About half an hour before you expect your first guest, uncover the bar, set out food and dips, check the bathroom, put on fresh lipstick. You're all ready to go. Have fun!

MENU

Cocktails   Highballs   Juice or Soft Drinks
Pâté*   Bleu Cheese Spread*
Raw Vegetables with Mustard Dip*   Cheese Balls*
Shrimp in Sauce*   Steak Tartare*
Marinated Mushrooms*   Spiced Olives*
Salted Nuts   Popcorn   Assorted Crackers

Eggnog Party

Somewhere between the High Tea and Cocktail Party lies the Eggnog Party. A wonderful way to entertain on a winter afternoon, it's especially nice during the Christmas holiday season when the house is decorated with evergreens, bayberry candles, mistletoe and holly.

Set the white-clothed, flowered-centered dining or serving table much as you would for tea, with a huge punch bowl of liquor-laced eggnog at one end and a bowl of plain eggnog at the other. You can ask friends to serve or let your guests help themselves.

Set punch cups, spoons, small plates and cocktail napkins near the punch bowls, and place platters and trays of food in between. Provide a side tray for used glasses. Eggnog is sipped from punch cups, but a spoon is needed to get the last of the thick mixture.

Eggnog should be smooth, rich and very cold. For maximum coldness, chill the bowls by heaping them with ice until just before the party begins. Then empty the melting ice, dry the bowls thoroughly and bring the eggnog directly from the refrigerator to the cooled punch bowl.

Serve cocktail-like sandwiches, but nothing really sweet—in combination with the eggnog, sweet foods would be cloying.

MENU

Eggnog*
Anchovy Sandwiches*   Turkey and Ham on Thin Rye Bread
Cream Cheese and Deviled Ham Sandwiches*
Fruitcake*   Salted Nuts

Sherry Party

For a late afternoon party in fall or winter, serve sherry. Offer a good medium sherry or give your guests a choice between a dry or cream sherry. Serve simple food, nothing rich, and decant the wine into the handsomest servers you have.

MENU

Sherry Wine
Cream Cheese on Nut Bread   Fruitcake*
Salted Nuts

Apéritif Party

For a more elaborate afternoon, plan an Apéritif Party with a choice of apéritifs accompanied by cheese, bread and crackers.

It's wise to have an extra supply of glasses on hand as many people like to sample several kinds. Leave the drinks in their original bottles for easy choice and serving.

MENU

Dubonnet   Pernod
Lillet   Cinzano
Sweet and Dry Vermouth
Cheese Board   Crackers   French and Rye Breads

Liqueur Party

Perfect for after-dinner is the Liqueur Party for which you offer various liqueurs and coffee.

Always have brandy and, since brandy is dry, have a sweet alternative. Again, provide extra glasses for those who wish to sample more than one kind.

MENU

Brandy	Cointreau
Green Chartreuse	Crème de Menthe
Benedictine	Drambuie
Coffee	

Italian Dinner

Do as the Romans do and spread a lavish Italian feast for your dinner guests.

Hang the walls with travel posters of Italy and scatter signs with Italian words and phrases. Stack records of Italian music on the record player and light the whole party area with candles stuck in empty Chianti and Italian vermouth bottles.

Instead of the usual hors d'oeuvres or dips, make an antipasto tray and serve it with Italian vermouth before dinner. Then send your guests around a buffet table centered with a paper gondola, some pieces of Italian glass and an arrangement of fruit and cheese. Serve several spaghetti sauces, letting each guest choose his favorite. Dessert comes from the fruit and cheese centerpiece.

MENU

Italian Vermouth   Grape Juice   Antipasto Tray*
Garlic Spaghetti Sauce* Meatballs and Tomato Sauce* Clam Sauce*
Tossed Green Salad   Parmesan Bread *
Radishes   Black Olives
Fresh Fruit in Season   Italian Cheese and Crackers
Coffee

Scandinavian Buffet

Food is king at any Scandinavian party, so be sure to have lots of it.

Informality is another byword, so serve buffet style, play Scandinavian folk tunes as background music (you can probably borrow the records at the public library) and plan a special table centerpiece.

Center the buffet table with a miniature Viking ship or create a Nordic forest of tiny artificial pine trees. If it's near Christmas, use the Scandinavian Christmas image of fruit on an evergreen base.

Use thin tapers, bright solid-color napkins rolled into standup cones, teak serving bowls and trays and stainless steel flatware. Provide card tables or individual tray seating to complete the relaxed atmosphere.

Two menus are suggested here. One is a smorgasbord, the other is based on an old Danish recipe called (appropriately for a wedding shower) Burning Love. Either will please your guests and further your reputation as an extraordinary hostess.

SMORGASBORD

Norwegian Meatballs*   Fish Balls*
Shrimp with Tomato Sauce Dip*   Sardines
Marinated Herring with Sour Cream Sauce*
Marinated Anchovy Fillets*   Boiled Potatoes   Pickles
Tossed Green Salad   Mushroom Salad*
Stuffed Eggs
Light and Dark Breads   Butter   Flavored Mayonnaise*
Assorted Cheeses
Aquavit, Beer, Coffee

Arrange fish foods at one end of the table, the meats at the other, with salads, relishes and breads in the center.

BURNING LOVE BUFFET

Burning Love Casserole*   Tossed Green Salad
Fresh Fruit Balls and Berries*   Norwegian Cookies*
Beer, Coffee

Oriental Buffet Dinner

Turn to the Far East for a dinner party to be remembered by even the most pro-Western minds.

Start with the decorations: raid your local import shop, Oriental district (if you have one) or the novelty section of a department store for paper lanterns, origami birds, paper parasols of all sizes, and serving dishes. Tack up panels of rice paper or bamboo patterned wall covering and use shiny paper-covered cartons for auxiliary serving tables.

If your food is to be Chinese, set the traditional round table that the Chinese favor, with bamboo place mats, and serve strong, hot tea throughout the meal, preferably in small, handleless cups. For a Japanese evening, offer your guests miniature cups of warm Saki wine and have them sit on the floor at small square tables.

Since Oriental cooking is not for beginners, it's a good idea to have your best local Chinese or Japanese restaurant cater the party. Check in advance on the menu. It's likely they will suggest ordering a variety of dishes "for the table" so each guest may have a sampling of as many different things as possible. Consult with them on timing, the serving setup and other details.

Hawaiian Luau

You can't take your guests to the Fiftieth State for a party, but you can still answer the siren song of the Islands by staging a colorful Hawaiian Luau at home.

A luau is an informal feast and if you can hold it outside so much the better. But indoors or out, it demands good food served in as authentic an atmosphere as you can muster.

Build a low table of planks set on kegs or blocks that is low enough so your guests can eat comfortably while seated on pillows or floor cushions. Cover it with a flowered cloth, use pyramids of fresh tropical fruit, candle hurricane lamps for light, and tuck ferns and flowers among the serving dishes.

Ask your guests to wear brightly colored Island style clothing and greet them with punch and *pupus* (appetizers) and fresh or paper flower leis. While you'll want to serve Hawaiian-inspired food, you may decide Mainland adaptations are safer. Both types are suggested here.

HAWAIIAN MENU

Pink Cloud Punch*   Tropical Punch*
Fried Shrimp and Sauce*
Chicken Chow Mein*   Coconut Sauce Fish*
Malihini Poi*   Hawaiian Fruit Salad*

Fresh Pineapple Sticks   Coconut Cookies
Coffee

MAINLAND-STYLE MENU

Baked Ham   Orange-Pineapple-Sauce*   Baked Sweet Potatoes
Hawaiian Fruit Salad*   Bread Sticks
Fresh Pineapple Sticks   Coconut Cookies
Coffee

Progressive Dinner

If several hostesses are giving the party and their homes or apart-
ments aren't too widely scattered, a Progressive Dinner will spread
the work and give the guests a different sort of party at the same
time.

One hostess is responsible for appetizers, another for salad, a third
for the main course and another for dessert and coffee. If you have
only three homes available, salad can be served with the main course
and perhaps two or three people can divide the work and expense of
this part. Serve salad before or after the main course, whichever is
the custom in your community.

If you have enough homes and your crowd would enjoy it, you can
go to still another house for drinks and dancing. In any case, shower
gifts are opened at the last house on the agenda.

Scheduling is of the essence for a progressive party, so write out a
time-and-motion chart in advance. Appoint one person to watch the
clock so the party segments don't overlap. Since this is usually a party
for a large group, buffet serving is best for all parts of the dinner.

In any event, all the food should be the kind that will wait, either
in the refrigerator or at low temperature in the oven, while the
hostesses all attend the rest of the party.

MENU

Individual Shrimp Cocktails*
Meat Loaf*   Green Bean Casserole*
Tossed Salad with Several Dressings
Hot Buttered Rolls
Pistachio-Bavarian*   Coffee

Cookout

The word cookout suggests the home magazine image of a charcoal grill on a spacious patio. If you have that kind of setup, fine. But don't let lack of facilities at home stop you. Take your party to the beach or park and either use their permanent stoves or grills or take along a portable charcoal grill and do your cooking on location.

Seat your guests at long picnic tables kept close together. Concentrate on color and utility—nothing formal or fragile belongs at this party—and be sure everything is firmly anchored. Set the table with a checked cotton cloth, colorful plastic-coated paper plates, stainless steel flatware and huge linen or paper napkins.

If it's an evening party, think about lighting: sink fat, slow-burning candles into sand-filled flowerpots, stick a patio torch or two in the ground and use hurricane lamps or kerosene-burning lanterns for the table. If you're at home, string outdoor Christmas lights with all-white bulbs and use floating candles in a birdbath.

You might decide to serve salad first while dinner is cooking on the grill, but you can serve it with the rest of the meal, with dessert later. Stack the plates beside the grill. Have the host (or cook) serve the meat, then hand the plate to the hostess (or assistant), who adds vegetables and salad. Pass bread in baskets and have another helper pour coffee and open canned beverages. Have several large plastic garbage sacks handy for constant cleanup.

MENU

Grilled Hot Dogs, Hamburgers or Steak
Foil-Broiled Vegetables*   Buttered Rolls or Onion Bread*
Tossed Green Salad
Seasonal Fresh Fruits or Fruit Roasted in Ashes*
Coffee, Beer, Canned Pop

Picnics

Even finicky eaters get hungry in the great outdoors, and man-size appetites become virtually uncontrolled. So when you pack your picnic basket, take plenty of food. What seems like more than enough will probably turn out to be only adequate, especially if you avoid the tired old sandwich-potato salad-cupcake routine in favor of a menu with more style.

Do the basic cooking at home, then reheat hot foods on a picnic stove or over a grill or bonfire. Unless you're sure of a safe water supply, take along jugs of chilled drinking water. Use an insulated ice carrier for keeping canned beverages cold and be wary of mayonnaise or seafood-based foods unless you can keep them positively icy.

Stick to easy-to-handle foods unless there are picnic tables at the site or you have your own portable table to set up. Rely on sturdy plastic-coated paper dishes and canned beverages, but bring along stainless steel cutlery. Plastic may be disposable, but it's a drag to use.

Take along ring toss, horseshoes, croquet or other games to play after dinner.

CAMPSITE PICNIC MENU

Chili   Oyster Crackers
Raw Vegetable Bowl*
Fresh Fruit in Season   Carrot Cupcakes*
Beer, Canned Pop, Coffee

If someone in the crowd has a station wagon, pull the tailgate down to cook and serve. Carry chilled cocktails, juice and soup in vacuum jugs and cook the meat on a portable grill. Serve soup in mugs and you won't have to contend with cutlery. But do have piles of dinner-size paper napkins.

TAILGATE PICNIC MENU

Cocktails   Chilled Vegetable Juice   Cheese and Crackers
Orange Beef Broth*   Hot Dogs or Wine Hamburgers* on Buns
Brownies   Coffee

Go the other way and add a touch of luxury by setting a picnic table with a fabric cloth and napkins, formal print paper plates, stainless steel knives, forks and spoons and glass and china for liquids. Serve buffet from a folding picnic table and set the places on the permanent table at the site—or carry two portable tables with you.

FORMAL PICNIC MENU

Cocktails   Porcupine Cheese Dip*
Cold Vichyssoise*
Teriyaki Marinated Steak*   Tossed Salad
Cantaloupe à la Mode
Red Wine, Coffee

If picnic site cooking is out of the question, don't panic. Picnic the way the French do. This simple, classic French outdoor lunch requires only a wineglass for each person and a sharp knife to cut the bread and cheese and spread the butter. What could be easier, or tastier?

FRENCH PICNIC MENU

Camembert or Cheddar Cheese
French Bread, Butter
Red Wine

Swim Party

Everyone into the pool—or the lake or the ocean—for a light-hearted Swim Party! If you have your own pool, then serving's no problem. But it's likely you'll have to transport the food to the party scene.

If you have access to an ocean or lake beach, you can come to dinner right from the water. But if you swim in a public pool at the park, a private club or the local Y, then pack lunch to eat later in a picnic area. Or if it's winter and you can use an indoor pool, come home later to feed the crowd on the living room floor which you've temporarily converted into an indoor beach.

Whatever you serve, be sure there's plenty because everyone will be hungry after swimming.

OUTDOOR AFTER-SWIM SUPPER MENU

Hot Dogs with Relishes   Savory Baked Beans*
Potato Chips   Tossed Fruit and Green Salad*
Date Roll*   Dixie Cups
Beer, Soft Drinks, Coffee

If you're eating at home, serve poolside or get your beach scene in the living room by spreading blankets, beach towels and beach cushions on the floor. Decorate with nets, cork or glass floats, seashells and cruise posters.

POOLSIDE MENU

Burgundy Stew*   or   Chili
Buttered French Bread
Fresh Fruit   Cheese and Crackers
Burgundy Wine   Coffee

Box Supper

This is one party where you do *all* the food preparation in advance. When serving time comes all you'll have to do is pass out the boxes, which should be stored in a cool spot, and pour coffee. Since everything will be finger food, you'll have almost no dish washing—just coffee mugs and a few spoons. If you use mugs, neither you nor your guests will have to cope with saucers.

Box suppers had their origin in frontier days when each girl brought supper for two in a specially decorated box, the frillier or more unusual the better. The men bid for the boxes, without knowing who had packed them, and chose their dinner partners in this way. For your party you'll probably want to pack one meal to a box and decorate them all alike. Your guests can eat right out of the box, even sit on the floor if they like.

Line each box with several layers of waxed paper and foil wrap each piece of food separately. Avoid drippy foods and include miniature salt and pepper shakers and sturdy napkins (linen or cotton are better than paper napkins for this meal).

Fried chicken is a favorite for box suppers. If you decide to serve it, use only legs, thighs and breasts, which are meatiest and easiest to eat. Provide plenty of garbage bags or other receptacles for discarded bones. Think about serving Hero Sandwiches, which are easier to prepare and a pleasant surprise.

MENU

Fried Chicken　　or　　Hero Sandwiches*
Deviled Eggs　　Celery and Carrot Slivers　　Pickle Spears
Cherry Tarts　　Salted Nuts
Coffee

Restaurant Party

If you can't manage a dinner party at home, take your guests to a restaurant. If you do some advance searching and planning, dinner out for a group need not be terribly expensive. Chinese restaurants, pizza parlors and small neighborhood restaurants can often provide an excellent meal at quite reasonable prices.

If you have facilities for entertaining on a limited scale, you can have everyone gather at your place for cocktails or a first course of soup sipped from mugs. Have the guest of honor open the gifts, then go in a group to the restaurant. Or you can have the guests come home with you after dinner and have the gift opening then. But if having people in is completely out, do the whole party in the restaurant.

Invite the guests as you would to any dinner. Give them the name and address of the restaurant and the time you want them to be there. Unless you can have a private dining room, give a group gift (if a gift is in order) to avoid attracting too much attention.

When the replies are in, go to the restaurant and make complete arrangements with the manager. Ask for a good table with candles and flowers (often a private room is available at no extra charge) and work out the menu. Arrange to pay for the meal, including tip, in advance.

Don't worry about the guests not being able to order individually. You would give them all exactly the same meal if you were serving at home, wouldn't you? Anyway, it's too confusing to have each person order separately and you can't take care of the bill in advance.

Arrive early to distribute place cards, check on the table and greet early arrivals. Then relax and enjoy your party in a way that the maidless hostess can't possibly manage.

Dessert Only

Pull out all stops when your party is for dessert only and load the table with a conglomeration of the fanciest goodies you can assemble.

Add fruit for dieters, a sweetmeat tray and some unshelled nuts and you'll have everyone agonizing over what to choose.

Depending upon the size of your guest list, serve some or all of the suggested desserts. Be sure to add any of your own specialties.

MENU

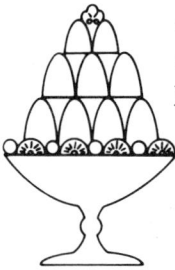

Cheesecake*   Dutch Apple Crisp*   Honeycake*
Chocolate Cream Roll*   Coconut Oatmeal Cookies*
Fresh Fruit Balls and Berries*   Sweetmeat Tray*
Bowl of Assorted Nuts in Shells   Coffee
Dessert Wine or Liqueur (Optional)

Cheese and Wine Tasting

If you can't manage dinner for a crowd and want something to substitute for a dessert party, a Cheese and Wine Tasting can be the answer to your dilemma.

Don't back off because you (or your guests) don't know a lot about wines or cheeses. Discovery is half the fun. Besides, no one should be expected to be a connoisseur, or even to venture an expert opinion. You'll learn by tasting and perhaps discover a lifelong affinity for a particular wine or cheese that you've never tried before.

There's a bit of ceremony connected with wine tasting that's fun to try. Pour a small amount of wine into a wineglass, then swirl it gently to catch the bouquet (fragrance). Sip slowly, rolling the wine on the tongue slightly to savor the taste. Then, before going to another wine, neutralize the taste by eating some bread and cheese.

The table will be the heart of the party, so set it where it will be accessible without blocking traffic. Have at least two wineglasses for each guest (one for red wines, another for white), plus some spares. Discourage clutter by not providing plates. Let the guests cope with the bread and cheese "as is."

Fashion a centerpiece by piling clusters of purple and green grapes into an enormous bowl flanked by hurricane lamps or outsize candles.

Group the wine bottles at one end of the table, whites and reds grouped separately, progressing from light to heavy. Set the cheeses on wooden boards and trays, each with its own spreader to avoid jumbling flavors, and choose bland crackers that won't interfere with the taste of the cheese. You might want to top some of the cheeses with miniature flags of their country of origin.

MENU

White Wines   Red Wines   Apéritifs
Danish Bleu Cheese   Liederkranz or Camembert
Gruyère   Swiss Cheese   Gouda
Sherried Cheese Spread*
French Bread   Rye Bread   Pumpernickel
Assorted Crackers   Plain Bread Sticks
Coffee

Evening Punch Party

Equally appropriate for either a couples or all girl party, an Evening Punch is simple yet fancy, easy to serve and thoroughly enjoyable for all.

Attention is centered on the refreshment table, which should have the most beautiful bouquet of fresh flowers you can manage. At one end of the table place a large bowl of Love Everybody punch, at the other have a smaller bowl of lemonade.

If you don't have punch bowls, don't fret. A deep dishpan carefully and smoothly covered with aluminum foil makes a handsome substitute.

Serve only finger foods so you won't have to bother with extra plates. If you're having men at the party, keep the sandwiches small, but not too fussy or dainty. If it's ladies only, be as feminine as you please. In either case, finish off the party with coffee and after-dinner mints.

MENU

Love Everybody Punch*   Lemonade with Floating Ice Ring*
Assorted Small Sandwiches*   Filled Celery*
Coffee   Mints

Late Night Supper

Perfect for a hungry horde, a Late Night Supper will send the crowd on its way happy and contented.

Since it's the last thing on the agenda, the food should be the kind that can be prepared in advance, then either kept hot or reheated just before serving so you won't spend half the party in the kitchen. Recruit enough helpers so you can whisk the food onto the table in an instant.

This party works equally well whether the group has been somewhere else and comes to your place for food, or whether they've been there all evening and are ready to be fed before heading home.

If it's an especially festive occasion go all the way with a superb chicken dish.

MENU

Champagne Chicken*   Wild Rice
Baby Peas   Tossed Salad with French Dressing
Petits Fours   Coffee

More down to earth, but still awfully good to eat, is this suggestion:

MENU

Corned Beef Casserole*   Swiss Green Beans*
Jellied Stewed Tomatoes*   Parmesan Bread*
Cupcakes   Coffee

Occasional Parties

Treasure Hunt

Everyone likes to play detective occasionally and if there's a chance at finding a treasure at the end of the trail of clues, so much the better.

In case you've forgotten, in a Treasure Hunt one clue, when unraveled, tells you where to find the next one until finally the chain leads the first person to find it to a special prize.

Don't spread the clues too far apart. Unless each couple has a car keep them within easy walking distance. Don't have too many clues, six or eight is plenty, and don't make them too hard to decipher or to find. Write them clearly on cardboard and pin them firmly in position, or hide them in covered bottles or jars nestled in tree forks or other spots where they won't be likely to be disturbed.

Don't pair husbands with wives or steadies with each other. Instruct everyone to wear walking shoes, to bring flashlights and to leave the clues where they find them so those behind them won't lose the trail entirely. Hide the "treasure" (perhaps a book, record or bottle of wine) near home, even inside the door or hall closet.

Since the guests won't all get back at the same time, don't plan to serve the food until the last straggler returns. It's a good idea, though, to greet the winners and early returnees with a drink or a cup of coffee.

Serve a make-your-own sandwich buffet or other late night supper and keep the treasure theme in the table setting: a doll trunk treasure chest overflowing with candy coins and dime store "jewels" as a centerpiece.

SCAVENGER HUNT

First cousin to a Treasure Hunt, the Scavenger Hunt is easier to plan. In this search all couples start with a list of crazy, hard-to-find items, and the ones who get back first with all (or the most) win the prize.

Set a time limit (an hour-and-a-half to two hours) and specify sternly that everything must come from home or friends—searchers are not allowed to buy *anything!*

Assign the guests as couples, but don't pair off spouses or steadies. Limit the list to common but not necessarily easy-to-find items—such as a marriage license, monkey wrench, baby doll or curling iron—and set a time for everyone to return, finished or not.

A buffet supper is good for this party. Center your table with a sampling of the items on the list to show that you could find them all —even though you had an unfair advantage.

Zodiac Party

It's in the stars that you'll have a successful party if you use a zodiac theme.

Write the invitations on zodiac stationery and use the astrology theme in decorating and serving: a crystal ball centerpiece surrounded by tarot cards and sprigs of juniper (juniper reportedly wards off evil influence), paper coasters and napkins with zodiac signs and horoscope place mats. Hang an astrology chart on the wall and provide a horoscope book so your guests can look up the predictions for their future.

If anyone in the group can read palms, tell fortunes from cards or otherwise read into the future, press their talents into service. You might even want to read up and try handwriting analysis or palm reading yourself. You can also letter ambiguous or funny fortunes on a dart board and let people spear their own fate.

This is a very flexible party for anything from a luncheon to an evening party for couples. So it's simply a matter of weaving the zodiac theme into your plans.

The prognosis? A heavenly party!

Around the World

If you like to travel, even if it's only the armchair way, take advantage of your interest in foreign lands to host an Around the World party, featuring food and decorations of the countries you have visited or would like to see.

Use in any combination: the brass bowls and table accessories of India, the flower leis and tropical fruit of Hawaii, the hot, bright colors of Mexico and Latin America, the voodoo dolls of the Caribbean, the cuckoo clocks of Germany, the wooden shoes and tulips of Holland, the red fez of Turkey, the straw mats and lacquer bowls of the Orient, the roses of England, the totem poles of Canada, the bamboo of the Philippines, the ivory and wooden carvings of Africa, the wool of Australia, the wine of France, the pasta of Italy and the leather of Spain.

Since this is such a personal party, no specific decorations or menus are suggested. Use your own imagination to set up a German beer garden, French sidewalk café, Oriental bazaar or whatever you like.

Make yours a one-country party or mix your décor and refreshments as much as your interests dictate.

Graduation

Graduation—to married life, parenthood, a new job or home—is a flexible theme that can be worked into almost any kind of shower.

Decorate with mortarboards, diplomas, books, pennants, horn rim glasses and other educational impedimenta—both the real thing and oversize drawings and sketches.

If most of your guests went to the same school, use the school colors for cup cake frosting. For a baby shower, make the frosting pink and blue, for a wedding shower use the wedding color scheme and for any other type of party make a spectrum of colors.

MENU

Vodka Punch*   Fruit Punch*
Diploma Sandwiches*
Frosted Cupcakes   Salted Nuts   Mints

Gay Nineties Holidays

The Battle of New Orleans, the Start of the California Gold Rush, Alaska's Admission to Statehood—these are only three of the special holidays that can profit by a Gay Nineties theme.

Set up an old-fashioned saloon, complete with a "free lunch" table. Decorate with old-fashioned portraits, heavily gilded mirrors, a player piano if you can get one (barroom piano records will do instead) and scatter some sawdust on the floor.

Provide steins or mugs for drinks, set out the food and let the guests help themselves.

If you like, fancy garters for the gals and derby hats or sleeve elastics for the men will add to the atmosphere. You might even have a few Barber Shop Quartet records to start everyone harmonizing.

MENU

Assorted Cold Cuts   Cheese Slices   Several Kinds of Bread
Butter   Mustard   Mayonnaise
Hard Boiled Eggs   Pretzels   Potato Chips
Whole Dill Pickles   Green and Black Olives
Beer   Root Beer   Coffee

Chinese New Year

Chase the post-Christmas holiday doldrums with a Chinese New Year's party.

The holiday falls on a different day each year, always near the end of January, and each year is named after an animal (The Year of the Dragon, The Year of the Rooster, The Year of the Dog, etc.). To find out the exact date and honored animal, check with the Chinese Consulate or Chinese Chamber of Commerce nearest you. If there is no Chinese community close by, enlist the aid of your local librarian. She can help you find the information.

Check the decorating and serving suggestions in the Oriental Dinner plan in this book and, if you can, follow the old Chinese custom of setting off firecrackers to welcome the New Year.

If you want to cook the dinner yourself, serve an Oriental version of an old American favorite, meatballs. For fun, provide each guest with a pair of chopsticks. But for practicality have a supply of forks in reserve.

MENU

Sweet and Sour Meatballs*   Rice
Sherried Bean Sprouts*
Tea and Fortune Cookies

Mardi Gras

This last blast, before the austerity of the Lenten Season begins, is traditionally given the night before Ash Wednesday. You may prefer to stretch the point a bit and hold it the preceding Saturday night so the festivities can go into the night without causing a conflict with weekday schedules.

This should be a costume party. In fact, insist on it, and serve the Country Style party menu that is a favorite with young couples in France.

Create a carnival atmosphere with clusters of balloons and festoons of crepe paper streamers in vivid hues of bright blue, purple, jade-green, yellow and red. Provide half masks—plain black for the men, and white or colored ones dusted with glue-based glitter for the women.

Cover the table with a red-and-white checked cloth, and use fat white candles everywhere.

FRENCH COUNTRY STYLE BUFFET MENU

Cheese Board*   Cold Sliced Ham   French Bread
Raw Vegetable Bowl*
French Mayonnaise*   Hot Mustard   Butter
Sangria Punch   Fruit Punch
Chilled Vin Rosé
Dried Fruits and Nuts

Mexican Independence Day

If your party falls on or near September 16, take inspiration from our neighbor to the south and celebrate Mexican Independence Day.

Use lots of flamboyant color everywhere, concentrating on hot shades of yellow, purple, pink and orange and the Mexican flag colors of red, white and green. Play recorded Mexican mariachi and folk music in the background.

Cover your table with a striped serape, use tan wrapping paper as a background for gaudy napkins or make a cloth of vivid striped material with solid color matching napkins. For the centerpiece load a ceramic burro or cart with small gourds, fill the brim of a small sombrero with tropical fruit or fill a woven basket with gourds. Use paper flowers, baskets, pottery and tiny cactus plants in profusion and hang a piñata over the table.

Cap the evening by blindfolding the guests and giving each a try at breaking the piñata with a stick. You can find piñatas at most import ships and in gift catalogs or you can make your own of papier maché (using a blown-up balloon as a base). Stuff it with dime store gifts and foil-wrapped candies. Serve a variety of Mexican food, then sit back and wait for the compliments.

MENU

Margaritas or Tropical Punch
Hot Bean Dip
Tamale Pie
Tostadas   Enchiladas
Melon Slices or Thawed Melon Balls
Coffee

Columbus Day

Since a shower honorée will soon discover a New World of Happiness, set the stage for the new life with a Columbus Day party theme.

Use the tools of discovery as decorating props: a telescope, old maps, coils of rope, a compass (have it pointing west), a ship's steering wheel, nail kegs for extra seating and a sign designating the bar as the Captain's Bridge. If you can't find some of these items, get an artist friend to draw wall-size sketches and hang them up.

Serve an Italian dinner, either the one below or the menu suggested in the Italian Dinner Party Plan, and drink an extra toast to old Chris—who gave you the inspiration for the party!

MENU

Italian Vermouth or Chianti   Grape Juice
Antipasto Tray*
Italian Soup*   Chicken Cacciatore*
Italian Green Salad*   Hard Rolls   Butter
Spumoni   Coffee

International Day of Bread

Women the world over still bake their own bread, at least for special occasions, and International Day of Bread (October 28) was established to encourage them to bake more often. Or any morning of the year this party could be a Bread Tasting instead of just a morning coffee.

Place loaves of different breads on cutting boards and let each guest slice her own. Don't alter the taste of the breads by offering jelly or jam. Just provide plenty of slightly softened butter, give each guest a small plate and a butter spreader and turn everyone loose to sample as they like.

You may want to serve some special bakery items, but be sure to bake at least some of the bread yourself.

MENU

Corn Bread*   Banana Bread*   Spice Bread*
Dinner Rolls*   Special Bakery Breads
Butter   Coffee

Christmas Tree Decorating

Let your guests share your Christmas by inviting them to a tree-decorating party. Sometime during the week before Christmas (Christmas Eve is often a good time) have the rest of the house decorated, the tree standing and the lights strung on it. Then invite your friends to help do the rest.

Have boxes of ornaments and strands of foil icicles at hand and delegate several persons to hang them in place. Give others bowls of popped corn and cranberries, big darning needles, spools of heavy thread and a thimble each and set them to stringing old-fashioned garlands to festoon the decorated tree.

Play Christmas carols in the background and urge everyone to sing along. When the tree is finished, place the shower gifts around it and after the couple has opened them serve a sandwich buffet.

MENU

Slices of Roast Beef, Chicken, Ham and Turkey
Slices of American and Swiss Cheese   Assorted Breads
Dill Pickle Rounds   Mustard   Mayonnaise   Butter
Fruitcake*   Coffee

Twelfth Night

January 6, or the evening of January 5, commemorates the visit of the Wise Men to Bethlehem and is a traditional time for many to take down the Christmas Tree.

If you want to leave your tree up that long after Christmas, have a Twelfth Night Party and let the guests help you take down the tree and pack the decorations to be stored until next year.

If possible, burn the tree outdoors. Otherwise, take it out of sight and dispose of it later.

In any event, serve the traditional Twelfth Night Wassail Bowl.

MENU

Wassail Bowl*   Mulled Cranberry Punch*
Fruitcake*
Fresh and Dried Fruits   Nuts in Shells

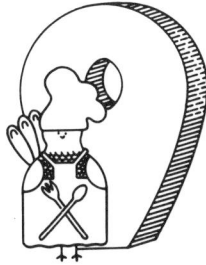

Recipes

Appetizers and Dips

ANTIPASTO TRAY

In making an antipasto tray, contrast flavors (spicy, sharp and bland) as well as colors. Choose at least six from the following:

sliced Gorgonzola, mozzarella, provolone or ricotta cheese
sliced prosciutto, salami or pork sausage
ripe, green, stuffed or pickled olives
raw green pepper slices
2-inch sticks of stuffed celery
deviled egg halves topped with anchovies
marinated mushrooms
canned artichoke hearts
lettuce, cherry tomatoes, radishes or scallions

Arrange on a tray flanked by a cruet of olive oil, a dish of lemon wedges, salad plates and forks. Let the guests serve themselves, then pass baskets of heated breadsticks and crackers.

INDIVIDUAL SHRIMP COCKTAILS

(MAKE SAUCE A DAY AHEAD)
1½ cups catsup
1½ cups chili sauce
3 tablespoons Worcestershire sauce
2 teaspoons freshly ground black pepper
1 teaspoon paprika
1½ teaspoons dry mustard
1½ teaspoons salt
3 or 4 dozen shrimp, cooked, shelled and deveined

Combine first 7 ingredients and refrigerate overnight in a covered bowl. To serve, place 4 tablespoons sauce in a demitasse cup with 3 or 4 toothpick-speared shrimp on the saucer. Or center a saucer with sauce in a small paper cup with shrimp surrounding it. (Makes 12 servings)

SHRIMP IN SAUCE

2 pounds shrimp, cooked, shelled and deveined
1 cup mayonnaise
¼ cup salad oil
3 or 4 tablespoons chili sauce (to taste)
1 teaspoon celery seed
1 clove garlic, minced
½ medium onion, chopped fine
1 stalk celery chopped
1 tablespoon dill seed

Combine ingredients and chill overnight. (Makes 8 to 10 servings)

MARINATED ANCHOVY FILLETS

1 can anchovy fillets (about 18 fillets)
2 tablespoons salad oil
1 tablespoon chopped chives or dill

Drain fillets and arrange on a small serving plate. Pour oil over fillets, sprinkle with chives or dill and chill several hours before serving.

MARINATED HERRING IN SOUR CREAM

While some specialty cookbooks have recipes for marinating herring, unless you're an expert it's safer to rely on the commercially prepared variety. Add a little more sour cream, a squirt of lemon juice and a few capers before serving.

STEAK TARTARE

1 pound lean sirloin steak, ground (have the butcher grind it especially for you so it will be fresh)
1 small-to-medium onion, grated (reserve juice)
1 teaspoon salt
¼ teaspoon freshly ground black pepper
1 tablespoon Worcestershire sauce
1 teaspoon capers
1 teaspoon caper juice

Mix all ingredients, including onion juice, thoroughly. Store covered in the refrigerator for about 12 hours. Serve mounded on lettuce, studded with capers, with thin slices of party rye bread for spreading.

CHEESE BALL

(MAKE AT LEAST 5 DAYS AHEAD)
½ pound soft cheddar cheese
1 (8-ounce) package Philadelphia cream cheese
5 ounces pimento cheese spread
3 ounces Roquefort cheese
1 tablespoon chopped parsley (more for rolling)
1 tablespoon Worcestershire sauce
¼ teaspoon powdered garlic
¼ teaspoon powdered onion
2 cups pecans, crushed

Bring cheeses to room temperature, then combine first 8 ingredients. Add ¾ cup pecans and blend thoroughly. Chill mixture until firm enough to roll into a ball or log. Shape and roll in mixture of chopped parsley and remaining crushed pecans until thoroughly covered. Wrap in transparent wrap and freeze for at least 24 hours. The day of the party thaw in refrigerator. Serve with crackers.

CHICKEN LIVER PÂTÉ

1 pound chicken livers, sautéed in butter
1 teaspoon ground cloves
1 teaspoon garlic powder
¼ teaspoon salt
¼ teaspoon freshly ground black pepper
1 bunch green onions
mayonnaise
8 slices bacon, fried crisp and crumbled

Grind liver and green onions (including tops) in food chopper with fine blade. Add other ingredients and mix thoroughly, using just enough mayonnaise to moisten the mixture so it will hold together. Form into a ball, roll in bacon bits and serve with assorted crackers.

SHERRIED CHEESE SPREAD

(MAKE AT LEAST 2 DAYS AHEAD)

1 pound sharp cheddar cheese, grated and warmed to room temperature
½ cup dry sherry wine
½ cup evaporated milk
½ cup butter
1 teaspoon salt
⅛ teaspoon cayenne

Mix all ingredients until smooth and creamy. Store in covered crock or jar. (Makes about 3 cups)

BLEU CHEESE SPREAD

(MAKE AT LEAST 2 DAYS AHEAD)

½ pound natural bleu cheese, grated
2 (3-ounce) packages Philadelphia cream cheese
¼ teaspoon Worcestershire sauce
¼ teaspoon paprika

dash salt
dash cayenne
3 tablespoons port wine

Let cheeses warm to room temperature. Combine with other ingredients in mixing bowl and beat with an electric mixer at high speed or with a rotary beater as fast as possible until smooth. Serve at room temperature for easy spreading. (Makes 1¾ cups)

FILLED CELERY

Wash and drain celery hearts. Fill with chicken salad, Philadelphia cream cheese and deviled ham, lobster or crab salad and prepared cheese spreads. Cut into 2-inch sections, cover with transparent wrap and refrigerate until serving time.

CHEESE STICKS

2 cups flour
½ teaspoon salt
6 tablespoons grated cheddar cheese
⅔ cup shortening
paprika

Sift flour and salt together. Cut in lard until well mixed and crumbly. Add cheese and mix well. Add a *tiny* amount of water, just enough so dough forms ball. Dough will be stiff. Chill thoroughly, then roll out until very thin (do not use extra flour to roll out dough unless absolutely necessary) and cut into strips. Sprinkle with paprika and bake at 450 degrees for 10 to 12 minutes.

CHEESE PUFFS

2 egg whites
¼ teaspoon salt
1 cup grated American cheese
1 teaspoon Worcestershire sauce
½ teaspoon paprika
½ teaspoon dry mustard
small rounds of bread, toasted on one side

Beat egg whites with salt until very stiff. Fold in cheese, Worcestershire sauce, paprika and mustard. Spread untoasted side of bread rounds with the cheese mixture and toast under a moderate broiler for about 6 minutes, until cheese is lightly brown and well puffed.

SPICED OLIVES

(MAKE A WEEK AHEAD)

half (8½-ounce) can ripe olives
1 (7½-ounce) jar pimento-stuffed green olives
2 cloves garlic, peeled and halved
2 bay leaves
1 teaspoon mustard seeds
¼ teaspoon thyme
¼ teaspoon salt
dash of freshly ground black pepper

Drain liquid from ripe olives and discard. Drain liquid for stuffed green olives and reserve. Arrange olives in a large jar and add spices, reserved liquid and water to cover. Refrigerate until needed.

MARINATED MUSHROOMS

2 pounds whole fresh mushrooms
⅓ cup vinegar
⅔ cup olive oil
2 teaspoons chopped chives
1 teaspoon tarragon
¼ clove garlic, finely minced
½ teaspoon salt
½ teaspoon sugar
½ teaspoon freshly ground black pepper
1 tablespoon lemon juice

Cut thin slice from bottom of each mushroom stem. Combine remaining ingredients in a covered jar and shake well. Place mushrooms in a bowl, pour marinade over them and let stand 24 hours. Drain and serve with colored toothpicks.

SUGARED PINEAPPLE AND STRAWBERRIES

Roll fresh strawberries and pineapple cubes or well-drained pineapple chunks in powdered sugar to coat thoroughly. Serve speared on toothpicks.

SPICED PINEAPPLE CHUNKS

(MAKE A WEEK OR SO AHEAD)

3 (#2½) cans pineapple chunks
2¼ cups vinegar
3½ cups granulated sugar
¼ teaspoon salt
18 to 24 whole cloves
3 (4-inch) cinnamon sticks

Drain pineapple chunks, reserving liquid. Combine liquid in sauce-pan with vinegar, sugar, salt, cloves and cinnamon and simmer un-covered 10 minutes. Add pineapple chunks and bring to a boil. Turn into a large bowl, cool and refrigerate for at least a week. Drain and serve on toothpick spears. (Makes about 24 servings)

SHRIMP WITH TOMATO SAUCE DIP

3 to 4 pounds large fresh shrimp
2 quarts water
1 quart beer
1 tablespoon salt
6 peppercorns
1 medium onion stuck with cloves
sprig of parsley

Split shrimp down the back with a pair of scissors. Remove the black veins but not the shells. Boil the rest of the ingredients together for 10 minutes. Add shrimp and cook for another 3 minutes. Remove shrimp from water and cool. Remove shells and serve with Tomato Sauce Dip.

TOMATO SAUCE DIP

1 cup heavy cream
½ cup condensed tomato soup
½ teaspoon salt
¼ teaspoon paprika
⅛ teaspoon ground cloves
½ teaspoon grated onion
¼ teaspoon dried basil

Whip cream until stiff. Fold in remaining ingredients. Serve in a bowl surrounded by shrimp. (Makes 1½ cups sauce)

RAW VEGETABLE BOWL WITH MUSTARD DIP

Heap in a large serving bowl any or all of the following:

    carrot spears
    cauliflower florets
    small whole fresh mushrooms
    green pepper sticks
    cherry tomatoes
    scallions
    young asparagus stalks
    celery spears
    red radishes
    cucumber sticks

Serve with Mustard Dip.

MUSTARD DIP FOR VEGETABLES

1 quart sour cream
⅔ cup Dijon mustard
1 teaspoon dry mustard
½ cup capers
2 tablespoons lemon juice
salt
chopped chives and parsley

Blend first 5 ingredients well, salt to taste and sprinkle liberally with chopped chives and parsley. Chill. (Makes about 4½ cups)

CRAB DIP

¼ pound cooked crab
1 pint Thousand Island salad dressing
½ cup mayonnaise
1 teaspoon lemon juice

Combine ingredients and chill. Serve with potato chips. (Makes about 2½ cups)

HOT BEAN DIP

2 cups kidney beans, drained, sieved and mashed
½ cup butter
¼ pound provolone cheese, cut in chunks
4 Jarapinos (tiny, hot green peppers) cut up fine
½ teaspoon Jarapino juice
2 tablespoons onion, minced
1 clove garlic, minced

Melt butter and stir in beans. Add cheese and stir until melted. Add peppers, pepper juice, onion and garlic and heat slowly. Serve hot with corn chips. This dip is quite piquant. If you prefer a milder version, reduce the number of Jarapinos. (Makes about 2½ cups)

GARLIC DIP

(MAKE 2 DAYS AHEAD)

2 (8-ounce) packages Philadelphia cream cheese
1 pint sour cream
8 to 10 garlic cloves, minced

Bring cream cheese to room temperature, then combine all ingredients thoroughly. Cover and store in refrigerator until several hours before serving. Serve with corn chips. (Makes about 2½ cups)

PORCUPINE CHEESE DIP

1 pound sharp cheese, shredded
¼ pound bleu cheese, crumbled
2 (3-ounce) packages Philadelphia cream cheese, softened
¼ teaspoon onion juice
½ teaspoon Worcestershire sauce
¼ teaspoon dry mustard
4 tablespoons milk
pretzel sticks

Blend cheeses thoroughly. Add onion juice, Worcestershire sauce, mustard and milk and beat until smooth and fluffy. Heap in a bowl, stud with pretzel sticks and serve at room temperature with extra pretzel sticks for dipping.

FRENCH VEGETABLE BOWL

1 red cabbage
green and black olives
dill pickle cubes
small white cocktail onions
cauliflower florets
artichoke leaves
green pepper strips
cherry tomatoes
raw mushrooms
cucumber slices

Center a large shallow bowl with the red cabbage studded with olives, pickle cubes and onions on toothpicks. Surround with as many as possible of the suggested fresh raw vegetables. Serve with French Mayonnaise as a dip.

FRENCH MAYONNAISE

1 egg yolk
hot French mustard in amount equal to egg yolk
peanut oil, at room temperature
salt and pepper

In a small bowl mix egg yolk and mustard. With the left hand pour peanut oil *very slowly* while stirring mixture steadily and evenly with a spoon in the right hand. Keep pouring oil (very slowly) and stirring constantly until mixture is a firm consistency, similar to very thick American mayonnaise. When mayonnaise is proper consistency, season with salt and pepper to taste. This is very difficult to make and takes practice. Perhaps at the beginning you should get a helper to pour the oil while you stir.

If mayonnaise falls or is too thin, try this: in a clean bowl put 1 tablespoon boiling water, then add sauce drop by drop, stirring constantly with a whisk, until it is the right consistency.

Serve as a dip for raw vegetables.

Soups and Sauces

ORANGE-BEEF BROTH

2 large navel oranges
3 tablespoons butter
2 (10½-ounce) cans beef consommé
1 soup can water
½ cup orange juice
1 teaspoon sugar
2 whole cloves

Using a vegetable peeler, cut 6 thin strips about an inch long from the outer skin of the oranges and reserve for garnish. With a sharp knife cut all the remaining peel, including white membrane, from the oranges. Working over a saucepan to catch all the juice, lift out the orange sections, discarding the peel. Add butter to the orange sections in the pan and simmer for about 3 minutes. Add consommé, water, orange juice, sugar and cloves, bring to a boil and simmer about 10 minutes. Strain, cool and refrigerate. Just before serving, reheat the clear broth, pour into mugs and garnish with a twist of orange peel. Serve piping hot. (Makes 6 small servings)

ITALIAN SOUP

1 (10½-ounce) can beef consommé
1 soup can water
3 egg yolks, well beaten
1 cup cream
oven toasted buttered French bread

Add water to consommé and heat thoroughly but do not boil. Using a wire whisk, stir in egg yolks, then cream. Simmer until hot through, but do not boil. Place toasted bread in soup bowl and pour soup over bread. (Makes 4 to 6 servings)

COLD VICHYSSOISE

Many cookbooks contain recipes for this French potato soup. However, there are excellent canned varieties which can be chilled at home and opened at the picnic site. Add a sprinkle of chopped chives.

ORANGE-PINEAPPLE SAUCE

2 tablespoons cornstarch
¼ cup sugar
2 tablespoons lemon juice
1 cup fresh orange juice
1 small can crushed pineapple
3 oranges, cut in bite-size pieces

Mix cornstarch and sugar. Add lemon juice, orange juice and liquid from crushed pineapple. Heat to boiling point, stirring constantly. Lower heat and cook until smooth and thick. Add pineapple and cook 5 minutes longer, stirring frequently. Add oranges and cook another minute or so. (Makes about 1 cup sauce)

FLAVORED MAYONNAISE

This fancy mayonnaise comes in tubes and can be found in many import or gourmet shops. If you can't locate it in a store, blend minced ham, crab or cheese into your favorite mayonnaise recipe.

HOT MUSTARD

Grey Paupon Dijon Mustard, imported from France, is available in many specialty food sections. If you can't find it, substitute American horseradish mustard.

Breakfast/Brunch Dishes

SCRAMBLED EGGS WITH MUSHROOMS

4 tablespoons butter
1 dozen eggs
½ teaspoon salt
12 tablespoons cream
¼ pound fresh mushrooms, sliced and sautéed in butter

Melt butter over low heat. Beat eggs, salt and cream gently until eggs are smooth and yellow. Add mushrooms and pour into skillet. When eggs begin to thicken stir constantly with a fork or wooden spoon until eggs are thick and slightly moist, not dry. (Makes 8 servings)

EMPRESS EGGS

8 eggs
4 tablespoons butter
1½ cups grated Parmesan cheese
2 medium onions, sliced into 8 slices ¼-inch thick

Melt butter in shallow baking dish and fry onion slices in it until golden brown. Remove from heat and sprinkle onion slices evenly with half the cheese. Carefully break an egg over each and top with remaining cheese. Bake in 350-degree oven until whites are firm. (Makes 4 to 8 servings)

PANCAKES

2½ cups sifted flour
5 teaspoons baking powder
4 tablespoons sugar
1½ teaspoons salt
2 eggs
2½ cups milk
6 tablespoons butter, melted

Sift together flour, baking powder, sugar and salt. Beat eggs lightly, then add milk and melted butter to egg mixture. Slowly pour liquids into flour mixture and stir just until mixed. Batter will be a little lumpy. Pour medium-size pancakes on a hot, lightly greased griddle or skillet and cook until bubbles appear in the cakes. Turn over to brown on the other side. (Makes 40 medium-size pancakes)

HOMEMADE MAPLE SYRUP

1 cup boiling water
1 cup white sugar
1 cup brown sugar
½ teaspoon maple flavoring

Pour water over sugar and stir until thoroughly dissolved. Add flavoring and stir again. Serve warm. (Makes about a cup of syrup)

DOUGHNUT HOLES

You can order these in advance from the bakers. To make your own, use your favorite doughnut recipe and cut the dough into ½- to ¾-inch circles.

Main Dishes

TERIYAKI MARINATED STEAK

(START PREPARATION 24 HOURS IN ADVANCE)

Bone and trim 7½ pounds chuck steak (meat will weigh about 4½ pounds afterward). Tie securely with heavy cord and marinate overnight in Teriyaki Marinade (see recipe following). Broil slowly over charcoal for 1½ hours, turning only once and basting occasionally with the marinade. Slice diagonally and serve. (Makes 8 to 10 servings)

TERIYAKI MARINADE

1 cup soy sauce
½ cup dry sherry wine
2 cloves garlic, minced
2 teaspoons sugar
2 tablespoons ginger root

Mix ingredients thoroughly. (Do *not* substitute powdered ginger for the ginger root as powdered ginger is quite different and will ruin the flavor.)

BURGUNDY STEW

2 pounds lean beef, cut into 1-inch cubes
2 tablespoons bacon drippings
5 medium onions, peeled and sliced
1½ tablespoons flour
generous pinch marjoram
generous pinch thyme
generous pinch salt
3 grinds fresh pepper
½ cup beef bouillon
1 cup Burgundy wine
¾ pound fresh mushrooms, sliced

Fry onions in bacon drippings until brown, and set aside. Sauté meat on all sides in same drippings, adding a little more fat if necessary. Sprinkle flour, marjoram, thyme, salt and pepper over meat. Add beef bouillon and wine, stir well and let simmer 3¼ hours over low heat (mixture should just bubble once in a while). If liquid cooks away add a little more bouillon and wine (1 part bouillon to 2 parts wine) to keep beef just covered. Add cooked onions and mushrooms and cook another hour, adding stock and wine if necessary. (Makes 6 servings)

WINE HAMBURGERS

1½ cups dry bread crumbs
1 medium onion, minced
¾ cup claret or Burgundy wine
1 egg, beaten
1 pound ground chuck
1½ teaspoons salt
¼ teaspoon freshly ground pepper

Pour wine over bread crumbs and add minced onion. When bread is soft, add the other ingredients, mixing well. Form into patties and brown in hot fat. (Makes 4 to 6 patties)

ITALIAN MEATBALLS AND TOMATO SAUCE

Sauce:

3 tablespoons olive oil
2 medium onions, sliced
1 clove garlic, minced
½ teaspoon basil
½ teaspoon oregano
1 (#2½) can tomatoes, strained through a sieve, including juice
1 teaspoon salt
⅛ teaspoon freshly ground pepper
½ teaspoon sugar

Fry onion and garlic in olive oil for about 5 minutes. Add basil, oregano and sieved tomatoes, stir well and simmer for about 45 minutes, stirring frequently. Add salt, pepper and sugar, stir again and simmer another 20 minutes. (Sauce for 8 ounces spaghetti)

(While sauce is cooking, prepare the meatballs.)

Meatballs:

1 pound ground chuck
3 tablespoons grated Parmesan cheese
2 tablespoons parsley, chopped
1 clove garlic, minced
¼ teaspoon dry mustard
1 teaspoon salt
⅛ teaspoon freshly ground black pepper
1 teaspoon Worcestershire sauce
1 cup fine bread crumbs
pinch of mace
¼ cup chopped onion
¼ cup chopped green pepper
2 eggs, beaten
3 ounces dry red wine
flour
3 ounces olive oil

In a mixing bowl combine first 14 ingredients thoroughly with your hands. Shape into balls about the size of an egg, roll in flour and brown in hot olive oil until golden brown, about 10 minutes. Nest meatballs on top of 8 ounces cooked thin spaghetti, pour on tomato sauce and serve. (Makes 4 servings)

GARLIC SPAGHETTI SAUCE

1 cup olive oil
5 garlic cloves, crushed
¼ cup fresh basil, chopped
½ cup fresh parsley, chopped
1½ cups water that has been used to cook spaghetti

Over low heat, brown crushed garlic cloves in oil. Stir in chopped basil and parsley and cook until parsley is slightly brown. Add drained spaghetti water and stir thoroughly. Strain the mixture and serve over cooked spaghetti. (Makes about 1¾ cups sauce)

CLAM SPAGHETTI SAUCE

⅓ cup olive oil
¾ cup finely chopped onion
3 (10-ounce) cans minced clams
1 teaspoon pepper
2 cloves garlic, finely minced
¼ cup chopped parsley

Cook onion in oil over low heat until soft but not brown. Drain clams and add liquid to onion. Cover and simmer over low heat for 15 to 20 minutes. Add clams, pepper, garlic and parsley and cook uncovered over moderate heat for 10 minutes, stirring occasionally. (Makes about 4 cups of sauce)

NORWEGIAN MEATBALLS

1 pound chuck, ground fine
½ pound pork, ground fine
1 egg, slightly beaten
1 tablespoon cornstarch
1 medium onion, minced
½ cup milk, scalded
⅛ teaspoon nutmeg
⅛ teaspoon allspice
⅛ teaspoon ground ginger
1½ teaspoons salt
¼ teaspoon freshly ground black pepper
4 tablespoons butter
1 tablespoon flour

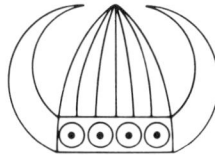

Combine meat, egg, milk and cornstarch, mixing well. Add next seven ingredients and beat until very light, then form into small balls. Brown in butter, then simmer slowly, adding a little water if necessary, for about half an hour, or until done. Remove meatballs from pan and add butter to drippings if necessary to make 2 tablespoons drippings. Blend in flour and brown, then slowly add enough water to make a medium thick gravy, stirring constantly. Put meatballs in serving dish and pour gravy over meatballs. (Makes 10 servings)

FISH BALLS

2 pounds salmon, codfish or halibut
milk
½ teaspoon salt
¼ teaspoon freshly ground black pepper
¼ teaspoon nutmeg
⅛ teaspoon mace

Remove the bones and scrape fish with a table knife. Grind through fine blade of meat grinder. Mix well, slowly adding milk until mixture will form balls. Add seasonings and mix well. Form into balls and fry in butter or shortening. (Makes 8 to 10 smorgasbord servings)

BURNING LOVE

Legend says that this recipe was originated long ago in Denmark by the bride-to-be of a Danish woodsman. She created it especially for him, and he was so impressed—both by the dish itself and the fact she had created it just for him—that he cut the heart-encased initials of his beloved on a tree trunk. Everyone who saw it knew he had carved it because of the "burning love" he felt for the girl and the dish she had created for him. Here's how to make it:

2 pounds of potatoes, cooked and mashed
1 teaspoon salt
⅛ teaspoon white pepper
3 tablespoons butter
1 pound canned Danish bacon
3 medium onions
2 cups cubed pickled beets
chopped parsley

Mash cooked potatoes with salt, pepper and butter. Dice bacon and onions and sauté in frypan until bacon is cooked and onion tender. Place mashed potatoes in a hot 2-quart serving dish and pour drained bacon and onions over the top. Garnish the edge with pieces of pickled beets and chopped parsley. (Makes 10 to 12 servings)

142

SWEET-AND-SOUR MEATBALLS

(CAN BE MADE AHEAD AND EITHER KEPT WARM OR REHEATED JUST BEFORE SERVING)

1 pound ground chuck
1 egg
2 tablespoons flour
½ teaspoon salt
¼ teaspoon freshly ground pepper
½ cup peanut oil
1 cup chicken broth
2 large green peppers, cut into small pieces
8 slices pineapple, cut in chunks
3 tablespoons cornstarch
1 teaspoon soy sauce
½ cup pineapple juice
½ cup vinegar
½ cup sugar

Shape meat into 16 small balls. Combine egg, flour, salt and pepper to make a smooth batter. Heat peanut oil in large skillet. Dip meatballs in batter and fry in hot oil until brown. Remove and keep warm. Pour out all but one tablespoon oil, then add ½ cup chicken broth, green pepper and pineapple. Blend remaining ingredients and add to skillet. Cook, stirring constantly, until mixture comes to a boil and thickens. Return meatballs to sauce and heat. Serve with hot rice. (Makes 4 or 5 servings)

MESCHOUI

This butter-basted roast lamb was brought to France from Algeria by French soldiers who served there.

Cook a large leg of lamb on the spit of a barbecue grill or rotisserie. Baste as the Algerians do by dipping the cloth-wrapped end of a stick in melted butter and smearing it on the meat as it turns. If you can't cook the meat on a spit, roast it in the oven, basting from time to time with melted butter. Either way, cook only until the lamb is rare to medium-well done. Carve a few slices and serve on cutting board, and ask the guests to cut their own portions as they like. Serve with French bread and butter.

BROCHETTES

When you order the leg of lamb for Meschoui, ask the butcher to include the lamb heart and liver. Cut them into bite-size cubes, alternate on skewers and broil, basting with butter occasionally, while the lamb roasts.

TAMALE PIE

2 cups white corn meal
1 teaspoon salt
5 cups hot water
2 (15-ounce) cans chili con carne without beans
grated sharp cheddar cheese

In double boiler combine corn meal, salt and hot water. Cook covered, stirring occasionally for half an hour or until it's fairly stiff. Start heating oven to 350 degrees. Heat chili con carne. Line bottom and sides of a 2-quart earthenware casserole with ⅔ of corn meal mixture. Pour in chili and dot top of chili with rest of mush. Bake 30 minutes. Just before serving sprinkle top of pie with grated cheese. (Makes 8 servings)

ENCHILADAS

1 (15-ounce) can red kidney beans
2 tablespoons butter
2 tablespoons minced onion
1 tablespoon chili sauce
1 teaspoon salt
1 pound ground chuck, crumbled and fried
1 cup grated cheddar cheese
1 can tortillas

Mash beans and strain. Mix with enough of the juice to make a paste. Cook onion in butter until soft, then add bean sauce, chili sauce and salt, and cook until creamy. In each tortilla place ⅛ of the ground beef and fold over edges so tortilla is divided in thirds. Place folded tortillas in a buttered shallow baking dish, pour on bean sauce and sprinkle with grated cheese. Bake at 350 degrees for 15 minutes. (Makes 8 servings)

TOSTADAS

2 dozen frozen, thawed, or canned tortillas
½ cup butter, melted
1 (15½-ounce) can refried beans, heated
2 pounds ground chuck, crumbled and fried
2 cups lettuce, finely shredded
2 cups sharp cheese, grated
bottled Mexican hot sauce

Fry tortillas in butter until golden brown. Drain. Spread beans on tortillas and top with ground meat, lettuce and cheese. Add 2 or 3 drops Mexican hot sauce. (It's *really* hot, so sprinkle cautiously!) (Makes 24 servings)

CHICKEN CACCIATORE

1 (3-legged) frying chicken cut into individual pieces
¼ cup olive oil
1 large onion, chopped
1 clove garlic, minced
1 (#2½) can tomatoes
1 carrot, sliced
½ cup dry white wine
1 teaspoon salt
⅛ teaspoon freshly ground black pepper
½ bay leaf
¼ teaspoon thyme
¼ teaspoon marjoram
½ pound fresh mushrooms, sliced
2 tablespoons brandy
1 teaspoon dried parsley

Sauté chicken, onion and garlic in olive oil until chicken is golden brown. Add remaining ingredients and simmer, covered, for 1 hour or until chicken is tender. Serve over spaghetti. (Makes 4 to 6 servings)

CHICKEN CHOW MEIN

1½ cups cooked chicken, chopped
3 tablespoons peanut oil
½ cup onions, thinly sliced

2 cups celery, chopped
1 cup green pepper, chopped
1 cup water
1 cup fresh mushrooms, chopped
½ cup almonds, chopped
½ teaspoon salt
6 tablespoons soy sauce
2 tablespoons cornstarch

Sauté onion in oil for 1 minute. Add chicken, celery, green pepper, salt, water and soy sauce. Cook for 5 minutes. Mix cornstarch with ¼ cup water and add to the mixture. Cook until thickened. Add mushrooms and almonds and cook 1 minute longer. Serve over crisp Chinese noodles. (Makes 4 to 6 servings)

COCONUT SAUCE FISH

2 cups hot milk
4 cups coconut, grated
salt
2 (1 pound each) red snapper or codfish fillets

Pour hot milk over grated coconut and let stand 30 minutes. Squeeze through double thickness of cheesecloth and discard coconut. Place fish fillets in greased baking dish. Salt lightly, pour coconut sauce (milk) over fish and bake at 350 degrees for 30 to 35 minutes. (Makes 4 to 6 servings)

MALIHINI POI

2 cups stale bread crumbs (no crusts)
2 cups milk, scalded
1 banana, mashed
2 tablespoons sugar
¼ cup butter, melted
½ teaspoon salt
2 eggs, slightly beaten

Soak bread crumbs in scalded milk and let cool. Add remaining ingredients. Bake in greased pudding dish for 1 hour at 325 degrees. When cool serve in small bowls. (Makes 4 to 6 servings)

CHAMPAGNE CHICKEN

(CAN BE MADE IN ADVANCE AND KEPT WARM)

10 to 12 large chicken breasts, boned and cut into bite-size pieces
¾ cup flour
1 teaspoon salt
⅛ teaspoon freshly ground black pepper
¾ teaspoon powdered ginger
1½ sticks butter
3 medium onions, quartered
3 carrots, quartered
2 bay leaves
3 splits champagne
3 cups heavy cream
1 pound fresh mushrooms, sliced

Sauté mushrooms in a little of the butter and set aside. Shake chicken pieces in a paper bag with flour, salt, pepper and ginger. In a Dutch oven, brown chicken in rest of butter, then add onion, carrot, bay leaves and champagne. Cover and simmer until chicken is tender (about 25 minutes). Discard onion, carrots and bay leaves. Add cream and mushrooms to sauce and heat without boiling. Serve on wild rice. (Makes 12 servings)

DEVILED CRAB

2 tablespoons butter, melted
2 tablespoons flour
2 cups cream
2 egg yolks
½ teaspoon salt
½ teaspoon cayenne
1 teaspoon mustard
1 teaspoon Worcestershire sauce
1 (6½-ounce) can crab, boned
½ cup mushrooms sliced and sautéed in butter

Blend butter, flour and cream in double boiler and cook 5 minutes, stirring constantly. Gradually add egg yolks, salt, cayenne, mustard and Worcestershire. Cook, stirring constantly, until thickened. Re-

147

move from heat, add crab and mushrooms and stir until heated. Serve in patty shells or on toast points. (Makes 8 patty shell servings)

MEAT LOAF

1¼ pounds chuck, ground
¼ pound pork, ground
¾ cup uncooked rolled oats
¼ cup onion, chopped
1½ teaspoons salt
¼ teaspoon freshly ground black pepper
1 cup tomato sauce
1 egg, slightly beaten

Combine all ingredients thoroughly. Pack firmly into an ungreased 8½ x 4½ x 2½-inch loaf pan and bake in a preheated oven at 350 degrees for 1 hour and 15 minutes. Let stand 5 minutes before slicing. (Makes 8 servings)

CORNED BEEF CASSEROLE

1 (10½-ounce) can undiluted cream of chicken soup
1 (10½-ounce) can undiluted cream of celery soup
1 cup half and half
¼ pound sharp cheese, diced
½ cup onion, chopped
1 (7-ounce) package small elbow macaroni, uncooked
1 (12-ounce) can corned beef, chopped

Mix all ingredients thoroughly. Turn into a 2-quart casserole, top with buttered bread crumbs and bake uncovered at 350 degrees for 1½ hours. (Makes 8 servings)

Vegetables

SHERRIED BEAN SPROUTS

½ pound fresh bean sprouts (or 1 (16-ounce) can bean sprouts)
3 green peppers
½ cup peanut oil
2 tablespoons sherry wine

148

1 teaspoon salt
1 tablespoon soy sauce

Cut peppers into thin strips about the width of bean sprouts and sauté in oil for 3 to 5 minutes. Add bean sprouts and cook another 3 minutes. Add sherry, salt and soy sauce, stir until mixed well and serve. (Makes 4 servings)

GREEN BEAN CASSEROLE

1 (16-ounce) can whole white onions, drained and marinated overnight in dry sherry wine
3 packages frozen French style green beans
2 (10½-ounce) cans undiluted mushroom soup
¼ pound fresh mushrooms, sliced and slightly sautéed in butter

Undercook by two minutes frozen green beans, using package directions. Drain and combine with other ingredients in a buttered 1½-quart casserole. Top with croutons, bread crumbs or Chinese noodles and bake uncovered at 350 degrees for 20 minutes. (Makes 8 servings)

GREEN BEANS WITH SWISS CHEESE

4 tablespoons butter
4 tablespoons flour
1 teaspoon salt
1 teaspoon sugar
½ teaspoon freshly ground black pepper
1 cup milk
1 teaspoon onion, grated
1 cup sour cream
4 (1-pound) cans small whole green beans, heated and drained
3 cups Swiss cheese, shredded
⅔ cup buttered crumbs

In a small saucepan, melt butter. Blend in flour, salt, sugar and pepper. Add milk, blend well and cook for 1 minute. Remove from heat and stir in onion and sour cream until well blended. In a mixing bowl, mix sauce with beans, then alternate layers of beans and cheese in a buttered 2½-quart casserole. Top with buttered crumbs. Bake at 400 degrees for 20 minutes. (Makes 8 servings)

SAVORY BAKED BEANS

1 (55-ounce) can baked beans
1 (5½-ounce) can pitted ripe olives
½ pound fresh mushrooms, sliced and sautéed in butter
bacon strips

Combine beans, olives and mushrooms thoroughly in a 2½-quart casserole or bean pot. Lay bacon strips across the top and bake uncovered at 325 degrees for 1½ to 2 hours, until thoroughly heated. (Makes 12 servings)

HARICOTS BLANCS (FRENCH WHITE BEANS)

1 pound Great Northern white beans (do not presoak)
1 large onion, quartered
10 slices bacon, cut into pieces, fried and drained
1 large onion, chopped
1 tablespoon tomato paste
1 (#303) can tomatoes

Cover beans with cold water, add quartered onion and boil gently for 2 hours. Be sure beans do not boil dry. Drain beans, reserving liquid. Combine cooked bacon, chopped onion, tomato paste and tomatoes with water from beans and simmer 20 minutes. Add cooked beans, mix well and cook another 10 to 20 minutes. (Makes 8 servings)

FOIL-BROILED VEGETABLES

Top an opened package of frozen vegetables with 4 tablespoons butter. Sprinkle with salt and pepper and wrap securely in double aluminum foil. Place on the grill and cook until tender (or bake in a 325-degree oven), about half an hour. Water from thawing vegetables will be enough to cook them. (Each package makes 3 or 4 servings)

JELLIED STEWED TOMATOES

2 (16-ounce) cans stewed tomatoes
2 envelopes unflavored gelatin
½ cup cold water

Empty tomatoes into a bowl, breaking up pieces slightly. Put water in top part of double boiler and sprinkle gelatin on water to soften. Place over boiling water and stir until gelatin is dissolved. Stir gelatin into tomatoes and mix thoroughly. Pour into 8 half-cup molds and chill until firm. Unmold and serve. (Makes 8 servings)

Salads and Salad Dressings

CRAB LOUIS

scant ¼ cup lettuce, shredded
½ cup crab meat
1 egg, hard-boiled and quartered
1 small tomato, quartered
4 ripe olives
4 carrot sticks
lettuce leaves

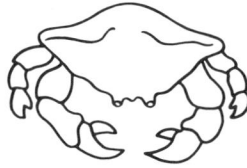

Arrange lettuce leaves on a luncheon plate. Make a bed of shredded lettuce and top with crab meat. Arrange egg and tomato quarters at sides and pour on ½ cup Sauce Louis. Garnish with olives and carrot sticks. (Makes 1 serving)

SAUCE LOUIS

1 cup mayonnaise
¼ cup heavy cream
¼ cup chili sauce
1 teaspoon Worcestershire sauce
2 tablespoons lemon juice

Combine all ingredients thoroughly and chill. (Makes about 2 cups sauce)

MOLDED SEAFOOD SALAD

2 (4½-ounce) cans shrimp
2 (3-ounce) packages lemon jello
2 (8-ounce) cans tomato sauce
1 cup sour pickles, chopped
1 cup celery, chopped
1 tablespoon India or sweet pickles, chopped

1 pint boiling water
salt to taste
1 cup walnuts or pecans, chopped (optional)

Combine all ingredients and pour into individual salad molds. (Makes 12 servings)

TOSSED FRUIT AND GREEN SALAD

2 heads romaine
6 slices bacon, cooked and crumbled
1 avocado, peeled and cubed
1 (11-ounce) can Mandarin oranges, chilled
2 green onions sliced fine, including tops
1 cup small cheese crackers
salt and pepper

Combine ingredients and toss with bottled Hawaiian style salad dressing. (Makes 8 servings)

ITALIAN GREEN SALAD

1 head lettuce
1 avocado, peeled and sliced
3 green onions thinly sliced, including tops
half an 8-ounce bottle Italian style salad dressing
1 teaspoon anchovy paste

Arrange avocado and onions over torn lettuce in a salad bowl. Add anchovy paste to salad dressing and toss with greens. (Makes 6 servings)

SALADE NICOISE

½ pound green beans, cooked until just tender
½ pound fresh tomatoes, quartered
½ pound boiled potatoes, diced
2 tablespoons capers
18 anchovy fillets

Combine ingredients in large salad bowl and mix with vinaigrette dressing until well blended. (Makes 6 to 8 servings)

MIX-YOUR-OWN SALAD

Provide bowls and baskets of various salad ingredients and invite your guests to assemble their own combinations. In addition to the basic lettuce, tomato quarters, cucumber rounds and radishes and green onions, try some of these:

dandelion or mustard greens
young spinach leaves
watercress
sliced fresh mushrooms
slivered almonds or chopped pecans
sliced hard-boiled eggs
croutons or cheese niblets
grated Parmesan cheese

Serve with a choice of salad dressings, including French and one with a cheese base.

HAWAIIAN FRUIT SALAD

(MAKE A DAY AHEAD SO SOUR CREAM AND MARSHMALLOWS WILL BLEND INTO A YUMMY DRESSING)

1 cup sour cream
1 cup coconut, shredded
1 cup pineapple tidbits, drained
1 cup Mandarin oranges, drained
1 cup miniature marshmallows
freshly ground nutmeg (optional)

Combine ingredients thoroughly and let stand overnight. Sprinkle with freshly ground nutmeg just before serving, if desired. (Makes 6 to 8 servings)

MACARONI SALAD

8 ounces elbow macaroni
1 (3-ounce) can chopped mushrooms drained
1 tablespoon onion, minced
¼ cup well-seasoned French dressing
¼ cup sour cream
2 tablespoons mayonnaise

1 teaspoon prepared mustard
1 teaspoon salt
⅛ teaspoon freshly ground black pepper
1 cup raw carrot, coarsely shredded
¼ cup diced green pepper

Cook macaroni according to package directions, drain and rinse. Combine mushrooms, onion, French dressing, sour cream, mayonnaise, mustard, salt and pepper. Then blend in carrot and green pepper. Mix with macaroni and chill thoroughly, overnight if possible. (Makes 6 to 8 servings)

CURRIED RICE SALAD

(MAKE A DAY AHEAD)

4 cups cooked rice
1 tablespoon vinegar
2 tablespoons olive oil
¾ teaspoon curry powder
¼ teaspoon salt
2 tablespoons pimento, chopped
¾ cup mayonnaise
1 package frozen asparagus spears, cooked (optional)

While rice is still warm, stir in vinegar, oil, curry powder and salt. Chill at least two hours, overnight if possible. Just before serving add pimento and mayonnaise to rice mixture, mix lightly and arrange in a mound on a large platter. Place asparagus spears around rice, if desired. If rice is chilled overnight, be sure to cover it tightly so it won't dry or get hard. (Makes 8 servings)

SOUR CREAM POTATO SALAD

6 medium potatoes, cooked just until tender, pared and cubed
1 pint sour cream
½ cup pimento-stuffed olives chopped
¼ cup black olives, chopped
¼ cup onion, chopped
1 teaspoon salt
¼ teaspoon freshly ground black pepper

½ teaspoon paprika
1 tablespoon parsley, chopped

Combine sour cream, olives, onion, salt, pepper and paprika and mix thoroughly with potatoes. Chill for several hours. Sprinkle with chopped parsley just before serving. (Makes 6 servings)

MUSHROOM SALAD

2 cups fresh mushrooms
1 teaspoon sugar
2 tablespoons cream
¼ medium onion, grated
⅛ teaspoon fine white pepper

Boil mushrooms in salted water until tender (about 3 to 5 minutes). Slice finely, add the rest of the ingredients and serve in a bowl or on a bed of lettuce. (Makes 8 to 10 smorgasbord servings)

MACARONI AND BLEU CHEESE SALAD

2 cups elbow macaroni
½ cup French dressing
1 cup sour cream
1 tablespoon vinegar
2 tablespoons mayonnaise
¼ teaspoon garlic salt
¼ teaspoon celery salt
¼ teaspoon freshly ground black pepper
¼ pound bleu cheese, coarsely crumbled
1 medium cucumber, peeled and diced

Cook macaroni in boiling salted water until tender. Drain and rinse. Mix with French dressing and cool. Toss remaining ingredients together and mix with macaroni. Chill. (Makes 4 servings)

FRUIT SALAD DRESSING

¾ cup sugar
2 teaspoons dry mustard
2 teaspoons salt
⅜ cup wine vinegar
⅜ cup lemon juice

3 tablespoons onion juice
2 cups vegetable oil (*not* olive oil)
3 tablespoons poppy seed

Combine sugar, mustard, salt, vinegar, lemon juice and onion juice in a mixing bowl. Add oil slowly, beating well until mixture thickens. Add poppy seed, stir and store until needed. (Makes 1 pint)

VINAIGRETTE DRESSING

½ teaspoon salt
½ teaspoon freshly ground black pepper
12 tablespoons olive oil
4 tablespoons vinegar
2 cloves garlic, peeled

In a small bowl combine salt, pepper and 2 tablespoons each olive oil and vinegar. Beat well with wire whisk until smooth. Add 4 tablespoons olive oil and beat well again. Add 2 tablespoons vinegar and 6 tablespoons olive oil and garlic. Place in covered jar and store in refrigerator. (Makes 1 cup)

Breads

BANANA BREAD

1¾ cups sifted flour
¾ teaspoon soda
1¼ teaspoons cream of tartar
½ teaspoon salt
⅓ cup shortening
⅔ cup sugar
2 eggs, well beaten
1 cup bananas, mashed

Sift together flour, soda, cream of tartar and salt three times. In a mixing bowl rub shortening with the back of a wooden spoon until creamy. Stir in sugar a little at a time and continue beating until light and fluffy. Add eggs, mixing thoroughly. Add a small amount of flour mixture alternately with bananas, beating until smooth after each addition. Pour into a well-greased loaf pan and bake at 350 degrees for 1 hour. (Makes 1 loaf)

SPICE BREAD

(MAKE A DAY AHEAD)

1 cup sugar
1½ cups boiling water
¾ cup honey
2½ teaspoons soda
¼ teaspoon salt
3 tablespoons rum
2 teaspoons anise flavoring
2 teaspoons cinnamon
4 cups flour, sifted

Pour boiling water over sugar, honey, soda and salt in a mixing bowl and stir until dissolved. Stir in rum, anise flavoring and cinnamon. Add flour gradually, stirring until smooth. Pour into 2 well-greased loaf pans and bake at 425 degrees for 10 minutes. Reduce heat to 350 degrees and bake an hour longer. Remove from pan and cool. When completely cooled, wrap in aluminum foil and store overnight. Serve in thin slices. (Makes 2 loaves)

CORN BREAD

2 tablespoons sugar
3 tablespoons shortening
¼ cup flour
1½ cup yellow corn meal
1 tablespoon baking powder
1 teaspoon salt
1 cup plus 2 tablespoons milk
1 egg

Heat oven to 450 degrees. Generously butter a 9-inch square pan and heat in oven while mixing batter. Beat egg, then all other ingredients and mix thoroughly. Pour evenly into heated pan and bake at 450 degrees for 20 to 25 minutes. (Makes 16 2-inch squares)

DINNER ROLLS

1 cake dry yeast
½ cup lukewarm water
2 teaspoons salt
1 egg, well beaten
½ cup sugar
½ cup melted shortening
1¾ cups lukewarm water
6½ cups all-purpose flour, unsifted

Soften yeast in ½ cup lukewarm water for 5 minutes. In a large mixing bowl combine softened yeast, salt, egg, sugar, melted shortening and 1¾ cups lukewarm water. Add flour a little at a time, beating thoroughly after each addition, until dough is stiff enough to knead. Knead on a lightly floured board until dough is smooth and elastic. Place dough in a greased bowl, cover with a warm, damp cloth and allow to stand 2 hours in a moderately warm place, turning the dough over occasionally. "Work down" (which translates "punch firmly once with your clenched fist"), cover tightly with foil and place in the refrigerator overnight. Before baking allow the dough to warm to room temperature (at least an hour). Form into desired shape, cover with a warm, damp cloth and let rise until treble in bulk. Place on a well-greased baking sheet and bake at 450 degrees for 15 minutes. If you don't use all the dough at once, it will keep covered in the refrigerator about a week. "Work down" daily to keep it from getting too light. (Makes about 3 dozen rolls)

ONION BREAD

soft butter
onion salt
loaf of French bread

Cut bread into ¾-inch slices almost to back of loaf. Butter each slice and sprinkle lavishly with onion salt. Wrap in aluminum foil and heat at 350 degrees for 20 minutes.

PARMESAN BREAD

½ cup soft butter
¼ cup grated Parmesan cheese

½ teaspoon savory
loaf of French bread

Combine butter, cheese and savory. Slice French bread in ¾-inch slices nearly to the bottom crust, but do not cut through. Spread butter mixture on slices, wrap in aluminum foil and heat at 350 degrees for 20 minutes.

ANCHOVY BISCUITS

1 package refrigerated ready-to-bake biscuits
5 flat anchovies

Split each biscuit halfway through the center. Cut flat anchovies in half and put half an anchovy in each biscuit. Gently press biscuit back into shape and bake at 400 degrees from 10 to 12 minutes, until biscuits are light brown on top. (Makes 10 biscuits)

SESAME-BUTTER STICKS

3 tablespoons butter
1 package refrigerated ready-to-bake biscuits
sesame seeds

Melt butter in 8-inch square baking pan. Roll each biscuit between palms of hands to make a stick 3 inches long. Roll in pan until well coated with butter, then sprinkle with sesame seeds. Bake at 475 degrees for about 10 minutes, until golden brown. Serve hot. (Makes 10 rolls)

Sandwiches

HERO SANDWICHES

8 slices salami
8 slices boiled ham
8 slices American cheese
8 slices Swiss cheese
16 slices fresh tomato, drained
1 Bermuda onion, sliced thin
shredded lettuce
olive oil
8 large hard rolls

Slice rolls in half lengthwise. On each roll layer one slice each salami, boiled ham, American and Swiss cheeses, 2 slices tomato and a few onion rings. Sprinkle with shredded lettuce and drizzle lightly with olive oil. If you serve them hot, omit lettuce, wrap in foil and heat in oven or on barbecue grill. (Makes 8 sandwiches)

PINWHEELS

2 (3-ounce) packages Philadelphia cream cheese
2 ounces Roquefort cheese
½ teaspoon salt
2 tablespoons sherry wine or Worcestershire sauce
1 loaf thinly sliced bread

Bring cheeses to room temperature and combine thoroughly with salt and wine or Worcestershire sauce. Cut crusts from bread and roll gently over each slice with a rolling pin. Spread each slice thinly with cheese mixture, roll up carefully, jelly-roll fashion, and fasten with a toothpick at each end. Place on a flat tray or cookie sheet, cover with transparent wrap and chill. Before serving remove toothpicks and cut rolls into thin slices with a sharp knife. (Makes 48 pinwheels)

SANDWICH TORTE

4 large bread rounds, lightly buttered
cream cheese and chopped nut spread
deviled ham spread
minced chicken moistened with mayonnaise

Trim crusts, then spread 3 bread slices with 3 different fillings. Top with fourth slice, butter side down. Press together gently, wrap in a damp paper towel, then in transparent wrap and refrigerate for several hours. Cut into pie-shaped pieces. (Makes 12 to 16 pieces)

CREAM CHEESE AND NUT SANDWICHES

1 (3-ounce) package cream cheese, softened
1 tablespoon walnuts, crushed
10 slices white bread, thinly sliced and lightly buttered

Combine cheese and nuts thoroughly. Spread on 5 slices buttered bread and top with remaining bread slices, butter side down. With a knife trim crusts, cut into quarters. (Makes 20 sandwiches)

ROLLED WATERCRESS SANDWICHES

1 large bunch watercress, washed and drained
¾ cup soft butter
¼ teaspoon salt
1 tablespoon lemon juice
1½ (1-pound) loaves white bread, thinly sliced

Remove stems from watercress, reserving center sprigs for garnish. Finely chop watercress to measure ½ cup. Beat butter and salt until smooth. Gradually beat in lemon juice, then chopped watercress. Trim bread crusts with a sharp knife. Spread bread slices evenly with watercress butter, using about 1¼ teaspoons for each. Roll up, jelly-roll fashion, then cut in half, securing with a toothpick if necessary. Refrigerate, rolled edge down, between damp paper towels until serving. Just before serving remove toothpicks and tuck a sprig of watercress in the end of each roll. (Makes about 50 sandwiches)

CREAM CHEESE AND OLIVE RIBBONS

1 (8-ounce) package Philadelphia cream cheese, softened
2 tablespoons mayonnaise
⅓ cup pimento-stuffed olives, chopped
½ cup butter, softened
12 thin slices white bread
12 thin slices whole wheat bread

Combine cream cheese, mayonnaise and chopped olives and blend well. Lightly butter 8 slices white bread and 4 slices wheat bread. Spread 4 of the buttered white bread slices and 4 of the buttered wheat bread slices with cheese mixture, using about 2 teaspoons for each slice. In 4 stacks, place wheat slices, cheese side up, on white slices, cheese side up. Top with 4 white slices, butter side down. With a sharp knife, trim crusts from each stack and cut each loaf into 6 strips (ribbons). Repeat with rest of bread and cheese mixture, this time with wheat slices on top and bottom. Arrange ribbons on a cookie sheet and cover with damp paper towels, then with transparent wrap. Refrigerate until serving time. (Makes 48 ribbons)

AVOCADO RIBBONS

2 cups avocado meat, mashed

½ cup mayonnaise
1 tablespoon lemon juice
1 teaspoon salt
dash of freshly ground black pepper
¼ cup parsley, minced
12 thin slices white bread
12 thin slices whole wheat bread

Combine avocado, mayonnaise, lemon juice, salt, pepper and parsley. Chill before spreading. Assemble as for Cream Cheese and Olive ribbons, but do not butter bread. (Makes 48 ribbons)

ANCHOVY SANDWICHES

Make a cup of your favorite egg salad recipe, using less mayonnaise than usual and chopping eggs extra fine. Add anchovy paste sparingly until you reach the taste desired. The paste is strong, so proceed cautiously. Spread on thin white bread slices, cover with another piece of bread, and slice into fingers. (Makes about 40 fingers)

CREAM CHEESE AND DEVILED HAM SANDWICHES

1 (3-ounce) package Philadelphia cream cheese
1 (4½-ounce) tin deviled ham spread

Soften cream cheese to room temperature. Add deviled ham, mixing until thoroughly combined. Spread on thin toast rounds, or spread on slices of thin bread, top with another slice of bread, trim crusts and cut into quarters. (Makes about 20 sandwiches)

ASSORTED SMALL SANDWICHES

Cut thin white, rye and whole wheat bread into rounds 2 or 3 inches in diameter. Butter lightly and spread half the circles with chopped egg salad, smoked salmon, chicken salad, Philadelphia cream cheese and deviled ham spread, avocado slices or minced ham salad and top with remaining buttered bread rounds. Cover with damp paper towels, then transparent wrap and refrigerate. When ready to serve, place on platters or trays and garnish with parsley sprigs.

DIPLOMA SANDWICHES

Make sandwich rolls as for pinwheels, but do not slice. Instead, serve in rolls "tied" in the center with a strip of pimento or curl of raw green pepper.

Desserts

FRUITCAKE

(MAKE 6 WEEKS IN ADVANCE)

1½ cups whole Brazil nuts
1½ cups walnut halves
1 cup pitted dates
1 cup chopped candied orange peel
1 cup each red and green maraschino cherries
½ cup seedless raisins
½ cup lime marmalade
¾ cup sifted flour
¾ cup sugar
½ teaspoon baking powder
½ teaspoon salt
3 eggs
1 teaspoon vanilla
⅓ cup sherry wine, brandy or rum

Grease a 9 x 5 x 3-inch loaf pan and line with waxed paper, which you grease again. Place fruit, nuts and marmalade in a bowl, sift dry ingredients together over them and mix well. Beat eggs in a small bowl until light and fluffy and add vanilla. Blend this mixture thoroughly into fruit, nuts and dry ingredients and spoon into pan, spreading evenly. Bake at 300 degrees from 1¾ to 2 hours, or until firm on top. Cool cake in pan for 10 minutes, then turn out on a wire rack, removing waxed paper. Sprinkle ⅓ cup sherry wine, brandy or rum evenly over cake, wrap in transparent wrap and store. Check in about 2 weeks and if the cake is dry sprinkle with another ⅓ cup sherry wine, brandy or rum.

HONEYCAKE

½ pound butter
1 cup brown sugar
1 cup white sugar
1 cup honey
3 eggs
1 cup sour cream
5 cups flour
1 teaspoon ground cloves
1 teaspoon cinnamon
1 teaspoon freshly ground black pepper
2 teaspoons soda

Cream butter. Add sugar, honey, eggs and sour cream. Beat well. Sift together flour, cloves, cinnamon, pepper and soda and add to mixture. Beat together thoroughly and pour into a greased and floured 9-inch square pan. Bake at 300 degrees for 1 hour.

APPLE CAKE

¼ pound butter
½ cup sugar
3 eggs
½ teaspoon lemon flavoring
pinch salt
2 cups flour
2 teaspoons baking powder
2 tablespoons milk
4 baking apples

Cream butter and sugar. Add eggs, lemon flavoring and salt, and beat well. Sift flour and baking powder together and add to mixture alternately with milk. Pour dough into a greased 10-inch (in diameter) round cake pan. Peel, core and quarter apples. Then with a sharp knife cut thin slices nearly to inside edge so apple quarters will fan out when cooked. Press apple sections, core side down, into the dough over entire cake surface and bake at 325 degrees for 40 to 50 minutes. (Makes about 8 servings)

INDIVIDUAL ICED CAKES

Bake your favorite white and chocolate cake recipes or mixes in sheets. Cut in 1-inch squares and, if desired, in diamonds, rounds and other fancy shapes with small cookie cutters. Frost with white, tinted and chocolate frosting and top with candy sprinkles, icing flowers, shaved semi-sweet chocolate and other decorations.

INDIVIDUAL WEDDING CAKES

Make your favorite white cake recipe or mix in sheets. Cut with round cookie cutters in 3-, 2- and 1-inch (in diameter) circles. Frost with white icing and assemble in 3 graduated layers. Top each cake with a silver foil leaf or pink frosting rose. (It's fun to bake foil-wrapped wedding cake charms into these small cakes: a dime for wealth, a ring for the next to be married, a thimble for the old maid and a wishbone for luck.)

CARROT CUPCAKES

4 eggs
2 cups sugar
1½ cups cooking oil
2¼ cups sifted flour
2 teaspoons soda
2½ teaspoons cinnamon
2 teaspoons salt
3 cups grated raw carrots

Beat eggs, add sugar, then beat in oil. Sift flour, soda, cinnamon and salt together and add to mixture. Add carrots last. Bake in greased or paper-lined muffin tins, filling cups about half full, at 350 degrees for 35 minutes. Frost with white icing. (Makes 30 to 36 cupcakes)

FATTINGMANN (NORWEGIAN COOKIES)

(MAKE DOUGH A DAY AHEAD)

10 egg yolks
5 tablespoons powdered sugar
½ cup heavy cream stiffly whipped
1 tablespoon brandy
1 teaspoon cardamon

½ teaspoon grated lemon peel
1½ pounds flour
2 tablespoons lard
powdered sugar

Whip egg yolks with powdered sugar. Add whipped cream, brandy, cardamon and lemon peel. Sift in flour and mix well. Allow dough to stand until next day. Roll out paper thin and cut in diamond shapes with cookie cutter. With a sharp knife, make a slit across the center of each cookie and pull one end through the slit. Fry in lard and sprinkle with powdered sugar. (Makes about 4 dozen cookies)

SESAME COOKIES

2 cups flour
1½ teaspoons baking soda
½ teaspoon salt
1 cup butter
1 cup sugar
1 egg
1 teaspoon vanilla
2 (2⅛-ounce) packages sesame seeds

Sift dry ingredients. Cream butter and sugar, then beat in egg and vanilla. Add sifted dry ingredients. Chill several hours. Roll 1 teaspoon dough at a time into a ball and roll in seeds. Place on a cookie sheet and bake at 350 degrees for 10 minutes. Cookies will flatten out as they bake. (Makes about 3½ dozen cookies)

COCONUT OATMEAL COOKIES

1 cup butter, melted
1 cup brown sugar
1 cup white sugar
2 eggs, beaten
2 cups flour
1 teaspoon soda
1 teaspoon baking powder
½ teaspoon salt
1 cup quick oats
1 cup wheat germ

1 cup coconut, shredded
1 teaspoon vanilla

Cream butter and sugar and add eggs. Sift flour, soda, baking powder and salt together and add to mixture. Add remaining ingredients, mixing well. Form into a loaf and chill. Slice about ¼-inch thick and bake until medium brown. (Makes about 3 dozen cookies)

CHEESECAKE

1¼ cups plain graham crackers, crushed
¼ cup butter, melted
1 (8-ounce) package Philadelphia cream cheese, softened
½ cup sugar
1 tablespoon lemon juice
½ teaspoon vanilla
dash salt
2 eggs
1 cup sour cream
2 tablespoons sugar
½ teaspoon vanilla

Combine crumbs and butter and press into buttered 8-inch pie plate, building up at the sides. For filling: beat cream cheese until fluffy. Gradually blend in ½ cup sugar, lemon juice, ½ teaspoon vanilla and salt. Add eggs one at a time, beating well after each. Pour filling into crust and bake at 325 degrees for 25 to 30 minutes, or until set. Combine sour cream, 2 tablespoons sugar and ½ teaspoon vanilla. Spoon over top of pie and bake 10 minutes longer. Cool, then chill several hours. Serve plain or topped with fresh or thawed frozen strawberries. (Makes 6 servings)

PISTACHIO-BAVARIAN

2 envelopes unflavored gelatin
1½ cups milk
½ cup sugar
6 egg yolks, slightly beaten
1 cup pistachio nuts, chopped
1 teaspoon vanilla
2 or 3 drops green food coloring

1 pint whipping cream, whipped
fresh or frozen strawberries

Soften gelatin in ½ cup milk. Combine remaining 1 cup milk, sugar and egg yolks and cook until thickened. Add nuts and vanilla. Add 1 cup of this hot custard to softened gelatin and stir until dissolved, then add remaining custard. When mixture starts to thicken, stir in food coloring and fold in whipped cream. Pour into a 3-quart mold and chill, overnight if possible. Serve topped with strawberries. (Makes about 18 servings)

DUTCH APPLE CRISP

4 cups apples (about 3), pared, cored and sliced
¾ cup sugar
½ teaspoon cinnamon
4 tablespoons water
3 tablespoons lemon juice
1½ cups graham cracker crumbs (17 crackers)
½ cup butter, melted
1½ cup sharp cheese, grated

Butter a 10 x 6 x 2-inch baking pan. Arrange apple slices in even layers in pan and sprinkle with sugar, cinnamon, water and lemon juice. Combine crumbs, butter and cheese and spread evenly over apples. Bake at 350 degrees for 30 minutes or until apples are tender and topping crisp. Serve warm, with cream. (Makes 6 servings)

CHOCOLATE CREAM ROLL

2 eggs, separated
1 cup sugar, sifted
4 tablespoons cold water
3 tablespoons cocoa
1 cup flour, sifted
½ teaspoon salt
1 teaspoon baking powder
powdered sugar
1½ cups sweetened whipped cream

With wire whisk beat egg yolks until thick and creamy. Mix cocoa and water and gradually add with sugar to egg yolks. Sift together flour, salt and baking powder and (still using wire whisk) add to egg mixture a little at a time, mixing well but not beating. Beat egg whites until stiff but not dry and add a little at a time to the batter. Grease a 17 x 10 x 1-inch pan and dust with flour. Spread batter very thin in pan and bake at 350 degrees for 10 minutes. Turn out immediately on a slightly damp cloth sprinkled with powdered sugar. Spread with whipped cream, roll up, jelly-roll fashion, (quickly but carefully) and wrap in cloth while still warm. When cool, remove cloth and sprinkle roll with powdered sugar. Cut into 1-inch slices. (Makes 10 to 12 slices)

DATE ROLL

(MAKE A DAY AHEAD)

½ pound miniature marshmallows
½ cup half and half
½ pound dates, seeded and cut into quarters
½ pound graham crackers, rolled fine
½ cup walnuts, chopped
1 cup sweetened whipped cream.

Drop marshmallows in cream, add dates and graham cracker crumbs and mix well. Place on waxed paper and shape into an 8-inch-long roll. Wrap waxed paper around roll and refrigerate at least 4 hours, preferably overnight. Serve in 1-inch slices topped with whipped cream. (Makes 8 servings)

FRESH FRUIT BALLS AND BERRIES

half a (13-pound) watermelon, cut lengthwise
1 quart fresh strawberries, washed and hulled
3 large oranges, peeled and sectioned
1 (12-ounce) can pineapple chunks
1 pound fresh berries or seedless grapes
1 cup water
½ cup sugar
1 tablespoon lemon juice
fresh mint sprigs (optional)

Scoop out watermelon meat in balls and place in large bowl. Remove excess liquid and seeds from watermelon and dry the inside well. Combine strawberries, pineapple and berries or grapes with watermelon balls. In another bowl mix water, sugar and lemon juice, blending well. Pour over fruit and stir gently but thoroughly. Chill well. Just before serving arrange fruit in watermelon shell and garnish with mint if desired. (Makes 12 to 16 servings)

If the fresh fruits are out of season, substitute thawed frozen fruits and berries served in attractive bowls. If you like, drizzle an ounce or two of brandy or cointreau over the fruit just before serving.

CANTALOUPE À LA MODE

Cut medium-size cantaloupes in half and remove seeds. Serve each half topped with a generous scoop of vanilla ice cream.

FRENCH FRUIT DESSERT

3 bananas, peeled and sliced
3 oranges, peeled and sectioned
3 apples, cored and sliced but not peeled
other sliced fruits in season
1 (16-ounce) can pineapple chunks, drained
1 (16-ounce) can fruit cocktail, drained
fresh lemon juice
scant ½ cup sugar

Sprinkle fresh fruits with lemon juice to avoid discoloration. Mix all fruits well, add sugar and stir again. Chill for several hours. If desired, add 2 ounces brandy with the sugar. (Makes 12 servings)

DRIED FRUIT AND NUTS

Arrange dried figs, apricots and prunes in a pyramid on a serving tray. Stud with assorted nuts in their shells and ring the tray with more nuts. Have a nutcracker and nutpicks handy and let the guests crack and shell their own as an accompaniment to the dried fruit.

FRUIT ROASTED IN ASHES

Roast fruit in barbecue ashes for a different taste treat. Wrap securely in double layer of aluminum foil and place in ashes. Turn once or twice during cooking and test for doneness by piercing through the foil, using a long-pronged fork.

ROASTED APPLES

Core apples and fill holes with sugar, cinnamon or nutmeg and a lump of butter. Wrap as directed above and roast for 30 minutes. Serve plain or topped with whipped cream.

ROASTED BANANAS

Peel bananas, dip in melted butter and sprinkle with sugar. Wrap as directed above and roast for 20 to 30 minutes. Serve topped with whipped cream or a drizzle of rum.

FRENCH CHEESE BOARD OR TRAY

Since there are over 850 different cheeses made in France and they don't export all of them, your offering will necessarily be representative rather than complete. You should have Camembert, Roquefort, Swiss, bombell, boursin and vache-qui-rit. You should be able to find most of them in import shops or specialty sections of the large supermarkets. Add your favorite American cheeses, and a round of gouda. If you can't find boursin cheese, our Philadelphia cream cheese is quite similar and an acceptable substitute.

Serve the cheeses on cheese boards and wooden trays with plenty of French bread and butter.

SWEETMEAT TRAY

Line a pretty tray with a cloth or paper doily and arrange sweets in separate sections. Provide spoons for serving candied peels and nuts. If you can make the candies yourself, fine. If not, go to the best candy store in town for:

Fudge   Divinity   Caramels
Assorted Chocolates   Candied Fruit Peel
Mints   Roasted Nuts

Drinks

TEA

Black teas are the most popular in this country. Consider Assam (robust), Ceylon (fragrant), Darjeeling (aromatic), Keemum (full-flavored but mild) or Lapsang souchong (distinctive, smoky-flavored) instead of the too familiar orange-pekoe.

For 50 cups, make in a large earthenware container with 30 teabags (or 30 teaspoons loose tea securely tied in a cheesecloth bag) with 7 quarts water. For smaller amounts use 1 teabag or 1 teaspoon of loose tea (in a tea ball) for each 2 cups.

To brew tea: start with cold water and bring to a quick boil. Warm a china or earthenware teapot by rinsing with boiling water. Put in tea and pour in boiling water. Cover and steep 3 to 5 minutes. Remove teabags or tea ball and serve.

COFFEE

To make coffee for a crowd, use a 50-cup urn if you can. Otherwise, keep several coffee makers going to ensure an adequate supply. A pound can of regular grind coffee will make 50 6-ounce servings. Don't try to save time or trouble by serving instant coffee. It just isn't as good.

Make the following variations with regularly brewed coffee:

Café au Rhum—add 1 ounce rum and a twist of lemon peel per cup.

Café Cacao—add ½ ounce crème de cacao per cup.

Café à L'Orange—add 1 ounce Orange Curaçao per cup with a cinnamon stick to stir.

Café Royal—place a cube of sugar in a coffee spoon. Pour on a generous splash of cognac and light with a match. When heat melts sugar, pour into coffee and stir.

Coffee à la Mode—add a spoonful of vanilla or coffee ice cream to the coffee as you serve it.

Café au Lait—pour equal amounts of hot milk and coffee into a mug, stir and serve.

Mocha Java—pour equal amounts of hot coffee and hot cocoa into a mug. Top with whipped cream and stir with a cinnamon stick.

Demitasse—serve coffee black in a small cup with cube sugar or a stick of cinnamon.

Viennese Coffee—float a dollop of whipped cream on top of coffee.

Iced Coffee—make double strength coffee and pour hot over ice cubes into thermal or metal glasses. Top with whipped cream and serve with straws.

IRISH COFFEE

True Irish Coffee is made with ⅓ Irish whiskey. This makes a mighty potent drink, so you'll probably want to cut the amount of whiskey to an ounce or so. Heat an 8-ounce glass or stemmed goblet by rinsing it with hot water. Pour in Irish whiskey (don't substitute another kind), add 3 spoonfuls raw sugar and fill with strong black coffee to within 1 inch of the brim. Stir to dissolve sugar and top off with slightly beaten whipped cream so cream floats on top.

ESPRESSO

Espresso is brewed from pulverized Italian dark-roast coffee. Some people use a drip pot, but for true continental style brew it in an espresso pot. Serve plain in a demitasse cup with sugar and a twist of lemon peel. Or try some of these variations, all of which start with an espresso base:

Caffè Cappuccino—pour equal parts of espresso and hot milk into a demitasse cup. Serve with sugar and sprinkles of cinnamon and nutmeg.

Roman Espresso—serve in a small wineglass with a twist of lemon peel.

Caffè Borgia—pour equal amounts of espresso and hot chocolate into a demitasse. Top with whipped cream and grated orange peel.

Caffè Cioccolata—pour equal amounts of espresso and hot chocolate into a taller-than-demitasse cup. Top with whipped cream, if desired, and shavings of French chocolate.

MEXICAN COFFEE

⅓ cup dark brown sugar, firmly packed
2 cinnamon sticks
½ cup ground coffee
4 cups water

Combine water, sugar and cinnamon in medium saucepan and bring to a boil, stirring until sugar is dissolved. Reduce heat and simmer, covered, 5 minutes. Stir in coffee and simmer uncovered another 2 minutes. Remove from heat, stir, cover and let stand until coffee grounds settle (about 5 minutes). Pour carefully into dinner-size coffee cups and serve. (Makes 4 servings)

LOVE EVERYBODY PUNCH

1 quart light rum
2 quarts gin
1 large bottle sparkling white grape juice
1 large bottle club soda

About an hour before the party begins, put a 10- or 12-inch block of ice into a large punch bowl and pour in the rum and gin. Just before serving, add sparkling white grape juice and soda, stir. If you need a second batch, be sure to put the liquor and ice in a bowl an hour before you need the punch. If you don't, it will be too strong— "Love Everybody" will turn into "Hate Everybody" and you'll have a hassle on your hands. (Makes 38 to 40 punch cup servings)

VODKA PUNCH

1 fifth Vodka
2 bottles sauterne wine
2 bottles ginger ale

Mix ingredients and serve in a punch bowl with lemon or lime ice ring. You can also float fresh strawberries or mint sprigs in the punch. (Makes about 35 punch cup servings)

SANGRIA PUNCH

(MAKE 24 HOURS AHEAD)

1 gallon red wine
4 oranges, sliced and quartered
4 apples, peeled, cored and sliced
½ lemon, sliced
1 cup sugar
1 tablespoon cinnamon
½ cup light rum

Mix ingredients thoroughly (preferably in a crock, but a punch bowl will do) and store overnight in a cool place. Do not refrigerate. The day of the party stir again, taste and, if necessary, add more sugar. Do not, however, make it too sweet. Add a block of ice or ice cubes about an hour before serving. (Makes about 35 punch cup servings.)

PINK CLOUD PUNCH

1 (6-ounce) can frozen red Hawaiian Punch concentrate
¾ cup water
¾ cup gin
1½ cups quinine water
2 tablespoons sugar
2 egg whites

Combine all ingredients in a large shaker and shake well. Pour over cracked ice in tall glasses, garnish with strawberries if desired. Serve with long straws. (Makes 6 tall drinks)

MILK PUNCH

5½ cups milk
8 eggs
8 teaspoons sugar
8 ounces whiskey or brandy
nutmeg

Beat milk, eggs and sugar with rotary beater until well mixed. Add whiskey or brandy, stir and pour into 8-ounce tumblers. Sprinkle with nutmeg. (Makes 6 servings)

EGGNOG

12 egg yolks
1 pound powdered sugar
1 quart dark rum, brandy or whiskey
2 quarts whipping cream
1 quart milk
6 egg whites
½ teaspoon salt
freshly grated nutmeg

Beat egg yolks separately until light in color. Then beat in powdered sugar gradually. Slowly add liquor, cream and milk, beating constantly. Refrigerate, covered, for 3 hours. Beat egg whites until stiff but not dry and fold lightly with salt into the other ingredients. Top each serving with freshly grated nutmeg. (Makes about 40 punch cup servings)

NON-ALCOHOLIC EGGNOG

For the non-drinkers serve a bowl of dairy eggnog which you can pick up in your supermarket.

WASSAIL BOWL

4 baking apples
¾ cup sugar
¼ cup water
3 cups ale or port
3 cups apple cider
1 teaspoon allspice

Core apples and sprinkle with ¼ cup sugar. Add water and bake at 375 degrees for 30 minutes (or until tender), basting several times with the syrup. Combine ale or port, cider, remaining ½ cup sugar and allspice in a saucepan and place over low heat. Stir until sugar is dissolved but do not boil. Put roasted apples in punch bowl and pour ale or port mixture over them. The true Wassail Bowl contains ale and it is recommended for this recipe, but you may substitute port if you prefer. (Makes 12 punch cup servings)

MAY WINE

2 bottles sauterne wine
¼ cup bar sugar
1 cup orange juice
1 cup fresh strawberries, sliced
2 oranges, sliced

Chill wine. Dissolve sugar in orange juice in chilled punch bowl. Add wine, sliced strawberries and orange slices. Float a few flowers on surface of punch and drop a small whole strawberry in wineglass just before serving. (Makes 15 punch cup servings)

CRANBERRY PUNCH

5 cups boiling water
5 teabags

¼ teaspoon allspice
¼ teaspoon cinnamon
¼ teaspoon nutmeg
¾ cup sugar
1 quart cranberry juice cocktail
3 cups water
1 cup orange juice
⅔ cup lemon juice

Pour boiling water over teabags, allspice, cinnamon and nutmeg and let steep for 5 minutes. Strain, add sugar and stir until dissolved. Let cool. Add cranberry juice cocktail, water, orange juice and lemon juice and mix. Put in punch bowl with Lemon Ice Ring or add ice cubes and float thin lemon slices on punch. (Makes approximately 25 punch cup servings)

FRUIT PUNCH

2 quarts strong tea, chilled
1 large can frozen orange juice, reconstituted according to directions on can
1 (32-ounce) can pineapple juice
1 large can frozen lemonade, *not* reconstituted
2 bottles ginger ale

Mix first 4 ingredients. Put in large punch bowl and add ice. Just before serving, add ginger ale and stir. (Makes approximately 30 punch cup servings)

TROPICAL PUNCH

Follow recipe for fruit punch, substituting a 32-ounce can of Hawaiian Punch for canned pineapple juice. (Makes about 30 punch cup servings)

MULLED CRANBERRY PUNCH

3 pints apple juice
1 pint cranberry juice
1 pint water
½ cup sugar
2 sticks cinnamon, cut into small pieces

20 whole cloves
20 whole allspice

Place cinnamon, whole cloves and whole allspice in a tea ball. Combine all other ingredients in a saucepan, add tea ball containing spices and simmer for 45 minutes. Remove tea ball and serve while punch is still warm. (Makes 20 punch cup servings)

LEMON ICE RING

Score 2 lemons with fork and cut into thin slices. Overlap slices on bottom of a 5½-cup ring mold and add water barely to cover fruit (about 1 cup). Freeze. Then fill mold with water and freeze again. Unmold and float in punch just before serving. Be sure to freeze fruit in small amount of water first to keep the fruit on the top of the ice ring where it can be seen. If you like, used scored limes or fresh whole strawberries and mint leaves instead of lemons.

Index to Showers and Parties

Index to Recipes